USN BATTLESHIP
VS
IJN BATTLESHIP
The Pacific 1942–44

MARK STILLE

Osprey Publishing
c/o Bloomsbury Publishing Plc
PO Box 883, Oxford, OX1 9PL, UK
Or
c/o Bloomsbury Publishing Inc.
1385 Broadway, 5th Floor, New York, NY 10018, USA
E-mail: info@ospreypublishing.com

www.ospreypublishing.com

OSPREY is a trademark of Osprey Publishing Ltd, a division of Bloomsbury
Publishing Plc.

First published in Great Britain in 2017

A CIP catalog record for this book is available from the British Library.

ISBN: PB: 978 1 4728 1719 8
            ePub: 978 1 4728 1721 1
            ePDF: 978 1 4728 1720 4
            XML: 978 1 4728 2418 9

18 19 20 21   10 9 8 7 6 5 4 3 2

Index by Rob Munro
Typeset in ITC Conduit and Adobe Garamond
Maps and diagrams by bounford.com
Page layouts by PDQ Digital Media Solutions, Bungay, UK
Printed in China through World Print Ltd.

Osprey Publishing supports the Woodland Trust, the UK's leading woodland
conservation charity. Between 2014 and 2018 our donations are being spent
on their Centenary Woods project in the UK.

To find out more about our authors and books visit
www.ospreypublishing.com. Here you will find extracts, author interviews,
details of forthcoming events and the option to sign up for our newsletter.

Author's acknowledgments
The author would like to thank Keith Allen for his review of the text which
resulted in several important improvements and clarifications.

Editor's note
All the photographs in this book are from the collections of the US Naval
History and Heritage Command. In most cases US customary measurements,
including US nautical miles (nm), knots (kts), and long tons, have been used in
this book. For ease of comparison please refer to the following conversion table:

1nm = 1.85km
1yd = 0.9m
1ft = 0.3m
1in = 2.54cm/25.4mm
1kts = 1.85km/h
1 long ton = 1.02 metric tonnes
1lb = 0.45kg

Title-page photograph: The longest-surviving battleship of the Imperial
Japanese Navy's Kongō class was *Haruna*, pictured after the war near Kure,
Japan. After a long wartime career, *Haruna* was hit on July 24 and 28, 1945 by
a total of 12 bombs from United States Navy carrier aircraft and settled in
shallow water.

Artist's note
Readers may care to note that the original paintings from which the
battlescene and cover artwork plates in this book were prepared are available
for private sale. All reproduction copyright whatsoever is retained by the
Publishers. All inquiries should be addressed to:

p.wright1@btinternet.com

The Publishers regret that they can enter into no correspondence upon
this matter.

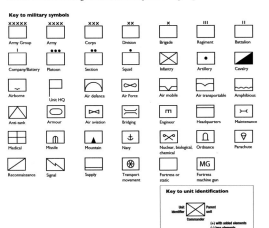

CONTENTS

INTRODUCTION

Going into the Pacific War, both the United States Navy (USN) and the Imperial Japanese Navy (IJN) foresaw a conflict which would be determined by a large-scale clash of battleships. It was not that both sides dismissed the roles of other fleet elements, but the mainstream consensus of American and Japanese admirals was that when the expected USN drive across the Pacific developed into a decisive battle and each navy's battle fleet was committed, battleships would play a central role and be the arbiter of victory. No other ship possessed the combination of long-range striking power and protection. The shared belief was that unless a battleship was exposed to torpedo attack by placing it in an unfavorable tactical situation, only a battleship possessed the power to disable or sink another battleship.

In this context, the role of aircraft carriers was considered secondary; they focused on scouting and providing protection for the respective battle fleets. Only a few naval-aviation zealots were bold enough to suggest that the development of the aircraft carrier and its aircraft was mature enough to usurp from the battleship the role as the centerpiece of the fleet. Before the war, both navies were heavily investing in air power, but both also kept increasing the size and capabilities of their traditional battle lines.

At the start of the war, the New Mexico-class vessels were considered the most capable of the USN's old battleships. For this reason, they were ordered into the Atlantic Ocean in 1941 to provide muscle to President Roosevelt's Neutrality Patrol. This view is of *Idaho* anchored in Hvaeldefjord, Iceland, October 1941.

As soon as it was permitted by the expiration of the London Naval Treaty in 1937, both sides embarked on a new battleship construction program.

When hostilities commenced, they did so in a way which clearly demonstrated the primacy of naval air power. The opening Japanese strike of the war was delivered at Pearl Harbor, Hawaii on December 7, 1941 by a force of aircraft carriers of unprecedented capabilities against the USN's Pacific Fleet battle line. Though the American battleships were caught unprepared in port, it was still clear that the aircraft carrier was now the most important component of a modern fleet by virtue of its mobility and long-range striking power. If there was any doubt that the battleship had been rendered obsolescent by air power, this was removed three days after the Pearl Harbor attack when Japanese land-based bombers sank a British modern battleship and a World War I-era battlecruiser off the coast of Malaya.

Both navies quickly adjusted to this new circumstance. Their battleships still had utility, but in a supporting role to aircraft-carrier task forces which now were the heart of each navy's battle fleet. If their speed allowed, battleships were incorporated into carrier task forces to increase the carriers' antiaircraft protection and to provide the muscle for surface task groups operating with the carriers to mop up cripples from carrier air attack or to seek surface engagement under the cover of friendly air power. However, within the context of carrier task-force operations, there was never an opportunity for either side's fast battleships to engage the other. The ranges at which carrier engagements were fought made it unlikely that battleships could be brought into play against their counterparts.

When forces from both navies were brought into close proximity of a mutual objective, such as defending or attacking a beachhead, the prospects for clashes between surface forces, which occasionally included battleships, greatly increased. This was the case around the island of Guadalcanal in the southern Solomons, which was the scene of a prolonged naval campaign from August 1942 until February 1943. Both the Americans and Japanese were initially reluctant to commit any of their few battleships into the confined waters around Guadalcanal, but as the campaign wore on, both had to reconsider. This was the scene of the first battleships duel between the USN and IJN during the war.

After an almost two-year hiatus during which no battleships were committed to an operation likely to include surface combat, the scene of combat shifted to the Philippines in October 1944. The American invasion of the Philippines prompted an all-out effort from the IJN to defeat the amphibious operations, including the commitment of its last nine remaining battleships. Against this, the USN had 12 battleships in action – six with the Fast Carrier Task Force and six with the invasion fleet. While the IJN's battleships remained largely inactive in home waters or at Truk Atoll in the Central Pacific, the USN's older battleships, too slow to operate with the carriers, were very active assisting the amphibious operations. In this capacity, the six old battleships assigned to protect the invasion of Leyte fought the last battleship action in history in October 1944. On both occasions in which American and Japanese battleships fought each other during the Pacific War, the USN emerged victorious, with technology playing a critical role each time.

Haruna and *Yamashiro* (at left) – representing the two oldest classes of IJN battleships in the Pacific War – photographed in the late 1930s. Unfortunately for the Japanese, these were also the only classes to face their USN counterparts during the war.

CHRONOLOGY

1913
August   *Kongō* is completed as a battlecruiser.

1914
August   *Hiei* is completed as a battlecruiser.

1915
April   *Kirishima* and *Haruna* are commissioned; *Fusō* follows in November.

1916
March   *Nevada*, the first USN "superdreadnought," is commissioned, followed by *Oklahoma* in May, *Pennsylvania* in June, and *Arizona* in October.

1917
March   *Yamashiro* is commissioned.
December   *Mississippi* and *Ise* are commissioned.

1918
April   *Hyūga* is commissioned.
May   *New Mexico* is commissioned.

1919
March   *Idaho* is commissioned.

1920
June   *Tennessee* is commissioned.
November   *Nagato*, the world's first 16in-gun battleship, is commissioned.

1921
July   *Maryland*, the USN's first 16in-gun battleship, is commissioned, followed by *California* in August.
October   *Mutsu* is commissioned.

1922
February   The Washington Naval Treaty is ratified; it requires the USN and IJN to decommission older battleships and places severe limits on the construction of new ones.

1923
August   *Colorado* is commissioned, followed by *West Virginia* in December.

1927–29
The Nevada-class battleships are modernized.

1929–31
The Pennsylvania-class battleships are modernized.

14in projectiles pictured on *New Mexico* while the battleship was replenishing ammunition prior to the invasion of Guam in July 1944.

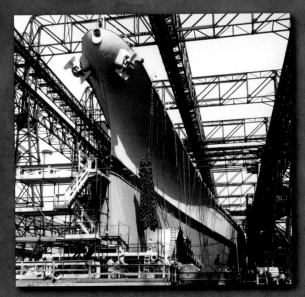

Iowa being prepared for launching at the New York Navy Yard in August 1942.

1930–35
The Fusō-class battleships are modernized.

1931–34
The New Mexico-class battleships are modernized.

1933–36
The Nagato-class battleships are modernized.

1933–37
The Kongō-class battlecruisers are rebuilt as battleships.

1934–37
The Hyūga-class battleships are modernized.

1941
April   *North Carolina* is commissioned, followed by *Washington* in May.

December   The Japanese attack on Pearl Harbor sinks *Arizona*, *Oklahoma*, *West Virginia*, *California*, and *Nevada*.

December   *Yamato*, the largest battleship ever built, is commissioned.

1942
March   *South Dakota* is commissioned, followed by *Indiana* in April, *Massachusetts* in May, and *Alabama* in August.

August   *Musashi* is commissioned.

November   *Hiei*, attempting to bombard the American airfield on Guadalcanal, is sunk by USN surface forces and aircraft. Two days later, *Kirishima* attempts a bombardment and is sunk by *Washington*. *South Dakota* is damaged in this engagement.

1943
February   *Iowa* is commissioned, followed by *New Jersey* in May.

May   The rebuilt *Tennessee* enters service.

June   *Mutsu* is sunk in a magazine explosion.

1944
January   The rebuilt *California* enters service, followed by *West Virginia* in June.

April   *Wisconsin* is commissioned, followed by *Missouri* in June.

October   At Leyte Gulf, *Fusō* and *Yamashiro* encounter a USN force led by six USN battleships and are sunk. *Musashi* is sunk by USN air attack.

November   *Kongō* is sunk by USN submarine attack.

1945
April   *Yamato* is sunk by USN air attack.

July   *Haruna*, *Ise*, and *Hyūga* are sunk by USN air attack.

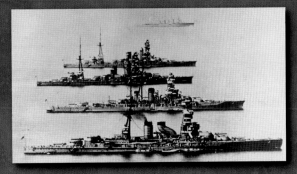

This view shows a substantial portion of the IJN's battle line in the 1920s. The battleship in the foreground is *Nagato*, behind her is the battlecruiser *Kirishima*, and the rear battleships are sister ships *Ise* and *Hyūga*.

DESIGN AND DEVELOPMENT

US BATTLESHIP DESIGN

When the USN entered the war in December 1941, it possessed 17 battleships, the largest fleet of such vessels in the world. In comparison, the IJN possessed ten battleships at the start of December 1941. The 17 USN battleships ranged from the pre-World War I *Arkansas, New York,* and *Texas,* to a series of so-called Standard-type battleships in five classes commissioned between 1916 and 1923, to the first of the "fast" battleships, *North Carolina* and *Washington,* commissioned in 1941. During the war, the USN commissioned eight more battleships: four South Dakota class and four Iowa class.

The three oldest USN battleships were part of the first generation of American dreadnought design. These possessed clearly inferior protection schemes and were obsolescent by the end of World War I; and by World War II they were seen as distinctly second-line units. The second generation of USN battleship design began with the Nevada class. These ships introduced several important features. The 14in/45 gun introduced on the Texas class was retained but mounted in only four turrets. Protection was significantly enhanced by the adoption of the "all-or-nothing" scheme. This replaced previous inefficient armor schemes which had attempted to protect almost all of a ship's hull with a new arrangement in which the available weight of armor was concentrated over vital areas, leaving large sections of the bow and stern unprotected. Also, the second generation of USN dreadnoughts moved to fuel oil, as opposed to coal.

Any battleship design has to balance the competing requirements of firepower, represented by its main and secondary batteries, protection, as defined by the coverage and characteristics of its armor, and speed, represented by the size and power of its machinery. Second-generation American dreadnoughts displayed the USN's preference for firepower and protection over speed. When the USN started building battleships again in 1937 after a 14-year hiatus, the balance between firepower, protection, and speed was improved. The development of more efficient machinery meant that in addition to being heavily armed and well protected, the third generation of USN dreadnoughts was also able to generate high speeds. This was critical because it meant that these battleships would be able to participate fully in the Pacific War, which had become dominated by fast carrier forces.

The Washington Naval Treaty of 1922 had an important influence on almost every class of USN battleship that saw action in the Pacific War. Most importantly, it limited the numbers of battleships that the USN could operate, which translated into a smaller battle fleet. With fewer battleships, the USN was less willing to risk them. The 15 battleships which the USN was allotted by treaty were limited to a certain tonnage and not allowed to upgrade their existing main battery. The existing battle fleet could not be replaced until it had reached retirement age (20 years), so existing ships were extensively modernized between the wars. In reality, modernization for the older ships was virtually a reconstruction.

Most of the 15 older USN battleships, except the Tennessee- and Colorado-class ships, received significant upgrades. Each ship kept its existing main battery, but the

This photograph was taken in the 1930s off Maui in the Hawaiian Islands, during the period when the battleship was still the centerpiece of the US Pacific Fleet. From right to left, a Tennessee-class, two Colorado-class, the other Tennessee-class, and one either Pennsylvania- or Nevada-class battleships are visible.

elevation of the turrets was doubled to 30 degrees, which resulted in much greater range. Protection was seen as their biggest weakness. To enhance underwater protection, upgraded ships received hull blisters which were designed to minimize hull damage by exploding a mine or torpedo at a standoff distance from the hull and letting the blister absorb the explosive energy. Horizontal armor was also increased to provide better protection against long-range plunging fire or aircraft bombs. When originally designed, the armor of the older battleships was designed to protect the vitals of the ships in gunnery duels at fairly short ranges. Engagements at shorter ranges meant enemy shells would strike the ship at low angles, which meant the main belt over the ship's hull was essential to provide protection of vital areas inside the ship. When fire-control systems improved and engagement ranges increased, the longer range meant shells would strike their targets at higher angles, making horizontal armor equally important. The USN addressed this problem by increasing the thickness of horizontal armor and by adhering to its innovative "all-or-nothing" protection scheme in which armor was concentrated only in areas which needed protection. This allowed thicker armor in those critical areas and helped control the overall growth in the ship's weight since armor protection was only required for a portion of the ship. Interwar reconstruction also upgraded the ships' propulsion systems, but the extra power gained only negated the effect of the hull blisters which created significant drag. As a result, even the upgraded battleships possessed a maximum speed of no more than 21kts, which restricted their operational employment.

The USN's first "superdreadnought," *Nevada*, photographed off New York in 1919. Note the mixed arrangement of the 14in/45 guns, with two triple and two twin turrets. *Nevada* was the last USN battleship to carry her main battery in this manner. The large cage masts were replaced by equally tall tripod masts by the start of the Pacific War.

THE NEVADA CLASS

When commissioned in 1916, this class of two ships, *Nevada* and *Oklahoma*, was the USN's first class of "superdreadnought," which combined a 14in/45 main battery with improved protection. The USN traditionally took an incremental improvement approach to battleship design, and the Nevada class was originally intended to be an upgrade of the preceding New York class. At the waterline, the Nevada class's hull was 575ft long; only 400ft of this was protected. Total weight of armor was 11,162 tons or 40 percent of the design displacement. The net effect was a ship better armored than comparable IJN battleships. Underwater protection was minimal, however – a common weakness of battleships of the day.

The main battery consisted of ten 14in/45 guns, but was mounted in only four turrets through the use of the USN's first triple turret. The secondary battery, which was designed to provide protection against torpedo attack by destroyers, initially consisted of 21 5in/51 single guns.

Between 1927 and 1929, *Nevada* and *Oklahoma* were modernized as described above. At the start of the Pacific War, both ships were caught in Pearl Harbor. *Oklahoma* was hit by five torpedoes and quickly capsized. The hull was raised in 1943, but the ship never returned to service. *Nevada* was hit by a single torpedo, but got under way, only to be hit by five 550lb bombs and beached. The ship reentered service with a new superstructure and greatly improved antiaircraft capabilities in time for the invasion of Attu in the Aleutians in 1943, and then moved into the Atlantic. The battleship returned to the Pacific for the invasions of Iwo Jima and Okinawa in 1945.

THE PENNSYLVANIA CLASS

This two-ship class introduced some important improvements from the Nevada class. The success of the two 14in/45 triple turrets fitted on the Nevada-class ships prompted the USN to fit four triple turrets on the Pennsylvania class, increasing the main battery to 12 14in/45 guns. The secondary battery initially consisted of 22 5in/51 guns, all fitted in casemates. Armor thickness and arrangement was similar to that of the Nevada class, but underwater protection was enhanced by the provision of a 3in-thick torpedo bulkhead fitted 9.5ft inboard from the outer hull. This was designed to withstand an explosion of 300lb of TNT.

Both ships underwent an interwar modernization beginning in 1929. Both were in Pearl Harbor on the day of the attack in December 1941. The fate of *Arizona* is well known. She was hit by two 1,760lb armor-piercing bombs; the second penetrated the horizontal armor forward and exploded in a propellant-charge magazine, starting a fire which spread to other magazines causing a catastrophic explosion. The entire forward section of the ship was shattered which precluded any possibility of salvage. *Pennsylvania* was in dry dock on the day of the attack so was spared any torpedo damage; the only damage was from a single 550lb bomb which was repaired by March 1942. From October 1942 through February 1943, *Pennsylvania* underwent a refit and modernization similar to that of *Nevada*. *Pennsylvania*'s antiaircraft fit was greatly enhanced, and 5in/38 dual-purpose guns replaced the 5in/51 casemated guns and the 5in/25 dual-purpose guns. From May 1943, *Pennsylvania* was active in a number of invasions of Japanese-held islands. As will be described later, she participated in the last battleship clash in October 1944 at the Battle of Surigao Strait.

THE NEW MEXICO CLASS

The next class of USN battleships, the three-ship New Mexico class, was laid down in 1915. These ships looked different from the Pennsylvania class with their clipper bows, but were virtually identical in terms of firepower and protection. The main battery was kept at 12 14in guns, but these were of the new 14in/50 type which possessed a slightly longer range. The redesigned gun turrets were completed with the capability of being elevated to 30 degrees. The secondary battery had 14 5in/51 casemated guns; these were placed higher up thus permitting them to be used in all types of seas. Propulsion on one ship, *New Mexico*, was altered to a turboelectric power plant which gave the promise of greater efficiency. This system proved successful and was adopted on the next class of battleships.

Between 1931 and 1934, the entire New Mexico class was extensively modernized. At the start of the Pacific War, this was the most modern class of USN battleships, with the obvious exception of the just-completed North Carolina class. The main and secondary batteries were unaltered, but the antiaircraft suite was increased. Protection was significantly increased with the addition of more horizontal armor and underwater protection was enhanced by the addition of a torpedo blister and a second torpedo bulkhead. New geared turbines were fitted, but maximum speed remained at a substandard 21kts because of the additional displacement.

When war came, the entire New Mexico class was in the Atlantic. All were shifted back to the Pacific in early 1942 to replace the battleship losses from the Pearl Harbor attack. Despite the fact that these were the most modern of the older battleships, none was sent to the forward areas. All were heavily used to support amphibious assaults and became very proficient in providing gunfire support to troops ashore. Because of this role, there was no time during the war for a major reconstruction. *Mississippi* and *Idaho* eventually had all their 5in/51 guns removed and *New Mexico* retained only six by war's end. All ships were fitted with fire-control radar, but this was dated by 1944. Only *Mississippi* was present at Surigao Strait.

THE TENNESSEE CLASS

This class of battleships, which consisted of *Tennessee* and *California*, was laid down in late 1916 and early 1917. In most respects, it was a repeat of the New Mexico class. The main and secondary batteries were unchanged in numbers or placement; and since the turboelectric power plant on *New Mexico* was successful, it was used for both ships of this class. In addition to the greater potential efficiency which could create a greater steaming radius (a promise which was not realized), the turboelectric drive did not take up as much space, thus allowing better internal subdivision. It was in protection that the new class displayed the most improvement with a further refinement of the underwater protection scheme. The New Mexico class introduced a torpedo bulkhead, and the Tennessee class went a step further by introducing a series of longitudinal splinter bulkheads between the double bottom to the lower armored deck. The spaces between the bulkheads could be left void or filled with liquids to absorb the blast from a torpedo or mine. The entire system created a depth of just over 17ft from the outer hull and was designed to withstand an explosion of 400lb of TNT. At the time, this was the most advanced underwater protection system fitted on any battleship and was the basis for all subsequent USN underwater protection systems.

Both ships were damaged by the Japanese attack on Pearl Harbor. *California* was struck by two torpedoes and a bomb. The torpedoes did not entirely defeat the underwater protection system, but progressive flooding caused by material condition issues caused the ship to settle on the bottom of the harbor by December 10. The ship was refloated in March 1942 and sent to the West Coast for reconstruction. *Tennessee* was struck by two 1,760lb bombs, but neither fully detonated so damage was light. The ship was quickly repaired and in August 1942 was released for a full reconstruction.

During reconstruction, both ships were rebuilt from the main deck up. The old superstructure was replaced with a new one based on the design of the South Dakota class. The main battery was retained, but was updated to accept automatic control and fire control was dramatically upgraded with the fitting of two Mk 34 main-battery directors, each with the Mk 8 fire-control radar. The old casemate-mounted secondary battery was removed and replaced with a battery of 16 5in/38 dual-purpose guns in eight twin mounts. Fire control was provided by four Mk 37 directors with the Mk 4 fire-control radar, the USN's most modern system for antiaircraft engagements. The antiaircraft battery was significantly upgraded with a profusion of quad 40mm mounts and single 20mm guns.

Protection was further enhanced with the addition of a torpedo blister and more internal longitudinal bulkheads. Horizontal protection was increased to a total of 7in of armor (8in over the magazines). Even after some equipment was removed to compensate for the extra weight, full-load displacement rose to over 40,000 tons. This extra weight meant that even the addition of new boilers which increased power could only drive the ship at a maximum speed of 20.5kts. Nevertheless, the modernization of these ships resulted in a battleship with combat capabilities approaching those of the USN's fast battleships. Reentering service in May 1943 (*Tennessee*) and January 1944 (*California*), the ships were a staple of major amphibious invasions and both were present at Surigao Strait.

This photograph is of *California* under way in Puget Sound in January 1944. The reconstruction was identical to that of *Tennessee* and gave the ship state-of-the-art fire-control and antiaircraft capabilities. The ship is painted in camouflage Measure 32 which was the favored scheme for all three rebuilt battleships entering service in 1944.

THE COLORADO CLASS

The three-ship Colorado class possessed the same protection schemes and propulsion system as the Tennessee class. The only major difference was the decision to move to a 16in/45 gun. The main battery still consisted of four turrets, but a twin turret was adopted, this reducing the main battery to eight guns. Because of the heavier 16in shell, the broadside of an eight-gun 16in main battery was virtually identical to the broadside from 12 14in guns.

All three Colorado-class ships were assigned to the Pacific Fleet at the start of the war, and two were in Pearl Harbor on December 7. *West Virginia* was moored directly in the path of the majority of Japanese torpedo bombers and took a probable seven torpedoes within minutes. Prompt counterflooding meant the ship settled on an even keel. *West Virginia* was raised in May 1942 and the following year she left for the West Coast for reconstruction along the lines of *Tennessee* and *California*. The work took until June 1944. *West Virginia* was at Surigao Strait and played an important role in the battle, as will be detailed later. The other two ships in the class, *Maryland* and *Colorado*, did not receive a major reconstruction during the war. Both were active during a series of amphibious invasions, and *Maryland* was present at Surigao Strait.

THE NORTH CAROLINA CLASS

After a 14-year hiatus, the USN laid down a new battleship in 1937. The maximum allowable displacement for a battleship per the Washington Naval Treaty of 1922 was 35,000 tons, and this was the limit used in the design work for the new class. The Washington Treaty expired in 1937, and was replaced by the Second London Naval Treaty. It stipulated a battleship limit of 35,000 tons and 14in guns, but had an escalator clause if other powers (in this case Japan) did not sign the treaty or commit to the limits. When Japan refused to commit to the 14in limit, an automatic gun-size escalator clause kicked in, raising the limit to 16in. Even as construction began, the design was being modified to accept a 16in main gun. For the main battery, a new type of lightweight 16in/45 gun was adopted. These were placed in three triple turrets with a maximum elevation of 45 degrees. For the first time on a USN battleship, the secondary battery was not placed in casemates; 20 5in/38 dual-purpose guns were used, placed in ten twin turrets with five along each beam.

Speed was a major design consideration and the design was criticized for sacrificing protection for speed. Advancement in machinery meant that power was raised to 121,000shp on four turbines, which was sufficient to drive the ship at a maximum speed of 28kts.

Protection suffered most from the requirement to design a ship within the 35,000-ton limit. Though it totaled some 41 percent of the design standard displacement, the scale of armored protection was actually less in some ways than the Standard battleships from the second generation of USN dreadnoughts. Horizontal armor was extensive with upper, main, and splinter armored decks. The underwater protection scheme built on previous designs and featured two additional bulkheads in addition to a torpedo blister. The machinery spaces were protected by a triple bottom for the first time.

By August 1942, *North Carolina* was in the South Pacific. On September 15, 1942, a Japanese submarine hit her with a single torpedo on the port side under the forward 16in/45 turret. The explosion caused a 32×18ft hole which placed her out of service until December 1942. This meant she missed the climactic surface battles in the Guadalcanal campaign. *Washington* began her war in the Atlantic, but by September 1942 she was in the South Pacific where she would play a major role in the November 1942 surface battles around Guadalcanal.

THE SOUTH DAKOTA CLASS

The consensus on the North Carolina class was that it was not as well protected as desired. This meant that when the USN was thinking about its next battleship class, it was decided to design an entirely new class rather than produce more North Carolina-class ships. This delayed the start of construction on the lead ship *South Dakota* until July 1939. For the new design, greater emphasis was placed on protection. USN designers traditionally believed that a battleship should have belt armor equal to the size of its main guns – so if the South Dakota class was fitted with 16in guns, the main belt

These are the two forward 16in/45 turrets on *Indiana* in an April 1942 photograph. Each turret weighed 1,437 tons and was heavily armored with 18in face, 9.5in side, 12in rear, and 7.25in roof armor. The USN's 16in/45 gun fired a 2,700lb armor-piercing or 1,900lb high-capacity shell.

15

needed to be 16in deep. However, since the design was still required to meet the 35,000-ton limit, it was a real challenge to balance the requirements of firepower, speed, and protection on such a relatively small hull. In the end the USN came up with a design with excellent characteristics in all three areas. As a result, the South Dakota-class vessels were probably the best of the treaty battleships designed by any navy.

The main battery remained at nine 16in/45 guns in three triple turrets. The secondary battery was also unchanged from *North Carolina* with 20 5in/38 guns in twin turrets. *South Dakota* was fitted as a flagship so had to sacrifice two 5in/38 twin mounts to compensate for the weight of a larger conning tower. The original design accepted a ship with a maximum speed of only 23–25kts. Fortunately for the USN, this was rejected because it would have been inferior to foreign, principally Japanese, designs. The final design speed was for 27.5kts which was achieved by increasing power to 130,000shp.

Protection was deemed adequate against 16in shells, but underwater protection was reduced. The main armor belt was 12.25in thick at the waterline, but it was internal to the hull and inclined at 19 degrees. Between the main belt and the hull, there were two torpedo bulkheads which created three compartments which were filled with fuel oil.

South Dakota was sent to the Pacific after completion, but hit an uncharted rock on September 6, 1942 and was forced to return to Pearl Harbor for repairs. She reached the area off Guadalcanal in October 1942 and took part in the Battle of Santa Cruz on October 26 where her intense antiaircraft fire claimed a reputed 26 Japanese aircraft. In November 1942, she returned to the waters off Guadalcanal and joined with *Washington*. The second ship of the class, *Indiana*, did not reach the South Pacific until late November 1942 and thus missed the last major surface battles of the Guadalcanal campaign. *Massachusetts* participated in the invasion of French North Africa in November 1942 where she engaged in a gunnery duel with the incomplete French battleship *Jean Bart*. *Massachusetts* reached the South Pacific in March 1943 and was followed by *Alabama* in September 1943. All four ships spent the rest of the war assigned as carrier escorts in the Fast Carrier Task Force and were not presented with any opportunity to engage IJN surface ships.

THE IOWA CLASS

The Iowa class – the largest and most powerful class of USN battleships ever completed – was the only class of modern USN battleships built largely free of the restrictions imposed by a naval treaty. The Second London Naval Treaty was technically still in place for much of the design process; this imposed a 45,000-ton limit – the signatories of the treaty, the United States, Britain, and France, had invoked an escalator clause in 1937 raising the limit from 35,000 tons – and a maximum of 16in guns, but the treaty was suspended with the outbreak of war in Europe. The design of the new battleship class represented a new approach for American naval designers. Previous USN battleships had clearly stressed firepower and protection over speed; the Iowa design placed speed as the design priority, though firepower and protection remained at high levels. The size of the new design – over 48,000 tons standard and over 57,000 tons full load – allowed for a truly balanced design.

The main battery of the Iowa class moved to the new lightweight 16in/50 gun. The main armament remained at nine guns in three triple turrets. The secondary battery consisted of the now familiar 20 5in/38 dual-purpose guns in ten turrets. In addition to firepower, speed was a primary design consideration. In order to reach the intended speed of 33kts, a massive increase in power was required. This was accomplished by fitting eight high-pressure boilers driving four shafts – the system was capable of generating a remarkable 212,000shp. Armor and underwater protection were similar to the South Dakota class and represented some 41 percent of the design standard displacement.

Four ships of this class were completed. *Iowa* and *New Jersey* entered service in 1943 and *Missouri* and *Wisconsin* the following year. Upon arrival in the Pacific, the ships were assigned to the Fast Carrier Task Force. In this role, they never had an opportunity to engage their IJN counterparts. The closest they came was on October 25, 1944 when *Iowa* and *New Jersey* were sent to cut off a Japanese force which included four IJN battleships (including *Yamato*) from retreating through the San Bernardino Strait. The intercepting USN force missed the Japanese by a matter of only a few hours, thus forever removing the opportunity to prove definitively which navy's most advanced battleship would have fared better in a battleship duel.

JAPANESE BATTLESHIP DESIGN

Throughout its history, the IJN had to prepare for conflict with opponents possessing larger fleets. The Japanese response in all cases was to build ships of the highest possible quality to compensate for any numerical inferiority. Once combined with an arduous training program, the IJN believed it had a winning formula to defeat its larger opponents.

This is a Kongō-class battlecruiser in its early configuration between 1917 and 1920. When completed, the ships had three stacks, two large tripod masts, and a very rudimentary bridge structure. All these features were altered during the course of many modernizations, but the arrangement of the main armament and the fact that all four ships of the class were lightly protected never changed.

This approach was evident during the run-up to the Russo-Japanese War that began in 1904. Before the start of the war, the IJN ordered six pre-dreadnoughts from British yards. The Japanese were not content to purchase copies of existing British battleship designs, however. The six ships were modified by the Japanese to produce faster, better protected, and better-armed warships which were among the best in the world at the time. These ships formed the IJN's battle line during the Russo-Japanese War and performed well, providing the backbone for the Combined Fleet's victory over the Russians. The crowning victory for the IJN was the Battle of Tsushima in May 1905. In this climactic encounter, the Japanese smashed a Russian fleet of 38 ships, sinking, capturing, or forcing into a neutral port for internment no fewer than 34 ships. This success cemented the notion of the decisive battle into the IJN's psyche. It also demonstrated the power of the battle line as the final arbiter of a naval clash.

Following the Russo-Japanese War, the IJN ordered a pair of pre-dreadnoughts built in Britain, each of which was fitted with four 10in guns in addition to the normal main battery of four 12in guns and a 6in secondary battery. A pair of semi-dreadnoughts followed, the second of which, *Satsuma*, was the first large warship to be built in Japan. They were considered semi-dreadnoughts because of their intermediate-caliber (8–10in) secondary battery. Construction of the first true IJN dreadnought commenced in January 1909 when *Settsu* was laid down. The two units of this class were fine ships with a main battery of 12 12in guns and a main armor belt of 12in – both were comparable to other dreadnoughts being built at the time, but their protection was noteworthy since only German dreadnoughts were similarly protected. Both ships were also fitted with turbine engines, making Japan only the third country to adopt turbines for large warships.

The IJN pressed for the fulfillment of its 8-8 Plan which it believed was the minimum level acceptable for national defense. The plan required a homogeneous battle line of eight battleships and eight battlecruisers. In 1910, despite a challenging economic environment, the Japanese government approved the construction of a class of four battlecruisers and one battleship.

THE KONGŌ CLASS

The four battlecruisers funded in 1910 became the Kongō class, and they had by far the most active and interesting career of any of the IJN's dreadnoughts. Built as battlecruisers before World War I, they were modernized between the wars and fought as battleships in World War II.

These ships began as a Japanese attempt to build a superior battlecruiser. The Royal Navy was the first to introduce the battlecruiser with the launch of *Invincible* in 1907, the idea being that an all-big-gun ship with a superior speed to battleships would confer tactical and strategic advantages. However, since all capital ship designs are a trade-off between the competing factors of speed, firepower, and protection, there was a price to pay for high speed. The route taken by the British was to sacrifice protection; and since the Kongō class was based on a British design, this was also the basic design emphasis for Japan's newest dreadnought – a class of high-speed battlecruisers with great firepower but only limited protection. After coming up with their own battlecruiser design, the Japanese decided to scrap it and seek British assistance in designing a much larger ship based on the 26,270-ton battlecruiser *Lion*. In 1910, an order was placed with the British shipbuilding firm Vickers for an improved 27,000-ton version of *Lion*.

The Kongō class totaled four ships. The first, *Kongō* – the last capital ship built for the IJN outside of Japan – was laid down in 1911 and entered service in mid-1913. The next ship, *Hiei*, was built in Yokosuka and entered service in mid-1914. *Haruna* was the first ship built with all-Japanese components at Kobe and was completed in early 1915. The final ship, *Kirishima*, was laid down in Nagasaki in early 1912 and completed in April 1915.

The basic design provided for a ship with high speed (27.5kts) and heavy firepower comprised of a main battery of eight 14in/45 guns in four twin turrets (all able to fire broadside) and a large secondary battery of 16 6in/50 guns. Protection was of battlecruiser scale with 6,500 tons of armor (25 percent of standard displacement) and a main belt of 8in at the waterline and 6in above it.

During their long careers, the Kongō-class battlecruisers underwent many modifications. Each ship went through two major modernizations during the interwar period, as did all IJN dreadnoughts. During the first modernization period (1927–32), an attempt was made to address the ships' principal weakness, namely their lack of protection. An additional 3,811 tons of armor were added to improve the horizontal protection of magazine and machinery spaces and underwater protection was increased with the addition of an antitorpedo bulge. The main battery was left in place, but the turrets were modified to increase maximum elevation to 43 degrees which increased their range. The original boilers were removed and replaced with modern ones.

The second modernization (1933–37) was more extensive and resulted in the ships being reclassified from battlecruisers to battleships. Horizontal protection was increased to a maximum of 4.75in over vital spaces and torpedo protection increased over the machinery spaces. The biggest improvement was in the new maximum speed of up to 30.5kts as a result of increasing the propulsive power to 136,000shp, this being achieved through the use of new boilers and turbines. The addition of 25ft on the ship's stern also helped increase speed. The main battery remained unaltered, but two of the 6in/50 casemated guns were removed in favor of a greatly expanded antiaircraft fit.

During the war, no major modifications were made. Since air attack was becoming the principal threat, the antiaircraft fit was greatly increased. In addition, six of the remaining 6in/50 casemated guns were removed by 1944. The two surviving ships received radar in 1943, but it is important to note that when *Hiei* and *Kirishima* were lost to surface action off Guadalcanal in November 1942, neither carried radar.

THE FUSŌ CLASS

The battleship authorized in the 1910 program became the lead ship of the two-ship Fusō class. The second ship, *Yamashiro*, was requested as part of the 1913 program. *Fusō* was built at Kure during 1912–15 and *Yamashiro* at Yokosuka during 1913–17. With this class, the IJN tried to design a battleship that was superior to any foreign adversary. The emphasis was on firepower, but protection and speed were also respectable.

The main battery was increased by 50 percent from that of the Kongō class. The six 14in/45 twin turrets were of the same type as on the Kongō-class ships, and all were able to fire broadside. This gave the two Fusō-class ships a comparable

This photograph shows *Fusō* after her modernization which began in 1930. She emerged as the ugliest ship in the IJN with her extremely ungainly pagoda-style forward superstructure. Note the catapult placed on top of the 14in/45 turret abaft of the superstructure; on sister ship *Yamashiro* which followed *Fusō* into the yards for modernization, the catapult was moved to the stern.

broadside to the latest USN battleships of the time. The arrangement of the guns, though, was inefficient and resulted in reduced arcs of fire. The retention of the midships turrets meant that the area to be protected was longer, which reduced the overall armor thickness. The secondary armament was 16 6in/50 guns, superior to that of USN battleships.

The propulsion system created 40,000shp, sufficient to drive the ships at 23kts through the water. This gave them a 2kts advantage over the USN's latest battleships.

Protection was improved over the Kongō class but was inferior to comparable USN battleships. The total amount of armor fitted was 8,588 tons, or some 29 percent of the ships' standard displacement. This was adequate for a main belt of 12in tapered down to 6in below the waterline. Overall, protection was inferior to the Nevada class which was its closest USN counterpart.

Just as with the Kongō class, the Fusō class underwent extensive modernization between the wars. *Fusō* was the first to enter the yards from April 1930 to May 1933. More armor was added for a new total of 12,199 tons or some 42 percent of standard displacement. This meant an increase in horizontal protection to a maximum of 5.1in. A torpedo bulge was also added.

The main armament was unaltered but its elevation was increased to 43 degrees, which bestowed a greater maximum range. Two of the 6in/50 casemated guns were removed and the elevation of the remainder increased to 30 degrees to increase range.

The propulsion system was entirely replaced with new boilers and turbines that resulted in a near-doubling of overall power to 75,000shp. This increase in power, combined with an extra 25ft on the stern to improve the overall hull form, meant that the Fusō-class ships' maximum speed was increased to 24.75kts, which increased their speed margin over USN battleships of the interwar period.

By the time of the Pacific War, the Fusō-class ships were the oldest and least capable of the IJN's battleships. Viewed as second-line units, little effort was made to modernize them and they were largely inactive during the first three years of the war. In September 1943, *Yamashiro* was designated as a training ship. Not until September 1944, with the war situation very much turning against Japan, were the two ships returned to active service. Both had their antiaircraft fit dramatically increased with light antiaircraft weapons and both were fitted with surface and air search radars.

THE ISE CLASS

The follow-on to the Fusō class was the two-ship Ise class that was approved in 1912 but not begun until 1915. *Ise* was commissioned in 1917, followed by *Hyūga* the following year. These two ships were intended as modified Fusō-class units but by the time they were completed, they were considered as a separate class because of the many improvements that had been incorporated.

The principal difference was a new arrangement for the placement of the midships 14in/45 turrets. The Ise class retained a main armament of 12 14in/45 guns in six twin turrets, but the two midships turrets were placed close together which resulted in a wider arc of fire. The secondary battery was increased to 20 guns, but these were the Japanese-designed 5.5in/50 weapon. Protection was on the same scale as that of the Fusō class. The better arrangement of the main battery permitted a more efficient

In the aftermath of the disaster at Midway during which the IJN lost four fleet carriers, work began to convert the two Ise-class battleships into hybrid battleship-carriers. The result is shown in this view of *Ise*. The hangar and short flight deck which replaced the two aft 14in/45 turrets had the supposed capacity to handle 22 aircraft; but the scheme proved completely pointless, and in 1944 both ships had their large catapults removed and fought as conventional battleships at Leyte Gulf.

placement of the boilers, which raised the output of the propulsion system to 45,000shp and a maximum speed of 23.5kts.

Despite the fact that both ships underwent a modernization during 1934–37 that was broadly similar to that given to the Fusō class, the Ise class was obsolescent when the Pacific War began. However, these ships were given a second career when the IJN decided to convert them into hybrid battleship-carriers in the aftermath of the defeat at Midway. The conversion was carried out in 1943 and basically called for the removal of the two aft 14in/45 turrets to be replaced by a 230ft flight deck serviced by two 82ft catapults. This would provide enough space to embark 22 dive-bombers. In the end, however, this awkward conversion was deemed impractical and not worth the time and resources devoted to it, with the result that neither of the ships ever embarked aircraft in combat.

THE NAGATO CLASS

The next class of IJN dreadnoughts marked another leap forward for Japanese naval architects whose goal was to design a ship qualitatively superior to any other navy's battleships. The principal advance was in firepower, the Nagato class having been designed to take the 16.1in/45 gun; when the lead ship *Nagato* was commissioned in November 1920, she was the world's first battleship to carry a weapon that large. The number of guns was reduced to eight, fitted in four twin turrets; but since they fired heavier shells, the eight-gun broadside was still comparable to that of previous classes armed with 12 14in/45 guns. The secondary battery was 20 5.5in/50 guns, all in casemates.

Another major advancement was the propulsion system which was entirely of Japanese design and manufacture. The 21 boilers and four turbines produced 80,000shp, sufficient to drive the ships at 26.5kts. The penalty for enhancements in firepower and speed was a stagnant protection scheme which despite accounting for 31.7 percent of standard displacement, produced only a 12in main belt.

As was customary for IJN battleships, both *Nagato* and *Mutsu* were modernized before the war. Horizontal armor was greatly increased over vital areas to provide protection from air attack and from plunging fire in a long-range battleship duel. Torpedo bulges were fitted. Though new machinery was also fitted, maximum speed dropped to 25kts because of the increased displacement. The main battery was unaltered, but the maximum elevation of the 5.5in/50 secondary guns was increased to add range.

THE YAMATO CLASS

The Nagato class was the last IJN battleship to enter service until 1941, a consequence of the Washington Naval Treaty of 1922 that placed a limit on overall Japanese battleship tonnage. The collapse of the naval treaty system in 1937, brought about by Japan, gave the IJN an opportunity once again to realize its desire to establish a qualitative edge in battleship design. Knowing that the USN could easily outbuild it in the absence of treaty restrictions, the IJN was determined to build a battleship which would overmatch anything the Americans were likely to produce. This desire resulted in secret plans to produce four superbattleships fitted with the largest guns ever placed on a battleship and protected with armor of unprecedented scale. The first

two ships, *Yamato* and *Musashi*, were authorized in 1936. Two more were approved in 1939, but were never completed as battleships.

Briefly described, everything about the Yamato class was massive. The main battery was nine 18.1in/45 guns – the largest ever mounted on a battleship. Speed was a very respectable 27.5kts achieved by means of a propulsion system capable of creating 150,000shp and through use of an innovative hull design. Most impressive of all was the scale of protection: quite simply, *Yamato* and *Musashi* were the most massively armored ships ever built, with a total weight of armor of 22,534 tons. An idea of the scale of protection can be gained by the fact that the main belt was 16in deep and inclined at 20 degrees, deck armor was between 7.9in and 9.1in, and the face of each of the three 18.1in/45 turrets was 26in thick. There were problems with the layout of the armor, but this was not revealed in a clash with USN battleships. Both ships were sunk by USN carrier air power – a threat barely imagined when these superbattleships were designed.

Yamato shown running trials on October 30, 1941. Her design and construction constituted a triumph of naval architecture and engineering. Despite the enormous investment made by the IJN in this class to gain a qualitative overmatch against American battleships, the only time *Yamato* used her 18.1in/45 guns in anger was against a USN escort carrier on October 25, 1944.

THE STRATEGIC SITUATION

At the start of the Pacific War, the IJN actually possessed a numerical advantage in battleships in the Pacific compared to the USN; a total of ten battleships in commission, with *Yamato* ready to join the fleet in mid-December 1941. Of these, only the four Kongō-class ships were employed during the first phase of the war: *Kirishima* and *Hiei* were assigned to escort the IJN's carrier strike force and *Kongō* and *Haruna* covered the invasions of Malaya and the Dutch East Indies. The remainder of the IJN's battleships remained almost exclusively in home waters until the anticipated decisive battle with the USN developed.

Of the USN's 17 battleships in service in December 1941, only nine were assigned to the Pacific Fleet. The three ships of the New Mexico class had been ordered to the Atlantic earlier in the year to support expanded USN operations in that theater. There they joined the three oldest and least capable USN battleships already in the Atlantic, *Arkansas*, *New York*, and *Texas*. The two ships of the North Carolina class were also in the Atlantic, but these were working up and were not yet fully effective.

The Pacific Fleet's battle line was caught in Pearl Harbor on December 7, 1941 and suffered heavily. Of the eight battleships present, five (*Arizona*, *Oklahoma*, *West Virginia*, *Nevada*, and *California*) were sunk, and the remaining three (*Pennsylvania*, *Maryland*, and *Tennessee*) damaged. Three of the five ships sunk were returned to service – *Nevada* in June 1943, and *West Virginia* and *California* in 1944 after reconstruction. Of the three ships damaged, none was out of service for long. *Pennsylvania* and *Maryland* returned to service later in December, and were joined by *Tennessee* in February 1942. (*Colorado* was on the West Coast at the time of the

Japanese attack, so was undamaged.) With the return of the three New Mexico-class ships in early 1942, the USN could muster seven battleships – a sharp contrast to the myth that the USN's battle line had been destroyed at Pearl Harbor.

The USN's re-formed battle line was not committed to front-line service throughout 1942 as the Americans fought to stem the Japanese advance. This was due to several reasons. Most importantly, the ships were too slow to serve in the carrier task groups which the USN quickly adopted as its primary striking forces in the aftermath of Pearl Harbor. In addition, the USN was short of oilers and destroyers to support and protect a battleship task force properly. In May 1942, the battleships were assigned to Task Force 1 and tasked to defend the West Coast against possible attack in the run-up to the Battle of Midway. In contrast, the Japanese were still looking for a decisive battle which would include a large-scale battleship duel. All 11 of the IJN's battleships, including the newly commissioned *Yamato*, were committed to the Midway–Aleutians

The attack on Pearl Harbor confirmed what many American and Japanese admirals already believed – the aircraft carrier had supplanted the battleship as the primary ship of both fleets. This is Battleship Row on December 7, 1941 after the Japanese attack. The sunken and burning *Arizona* is in the center. To the left are *Tennessee* and the sunken *West Virginia*.

operation in June 1942. The culmination of this operation was planned to be a decisive fleet action in which all the non-Kongō-class Japanese battleships would form up into a single formation to engage the remnants of the USN, including battleships, which would be lured to Midway to be destroyed. Such an unrealistic plan had no chance of success. The USN had no intention of bringing its re-formed battle line into play, but instead deployed three carriers to ambush the Japanese carrier force. The American ambush was successful, sinking four Japanese fleet carriers, and the IJN's imposing battle line contributed nothing.

After the Battle of Midway, the focus of naval operations shifted to the South Pacific when the Americans landed on Guadalcanal on August 8, 1942. By this time, *North Carolina* had reached the Pacific, and was assigned to the carrier task force. The campaign became a prolonged attritional contest in which control of Henderson Field (the airfield on Guadalcanal) was vital. A series of night surface actions were fought around Guadalcanal as the USN attempted to prevent Japanese reinforcements from reaching the island. Both sides committed heavy and light cruisers, escorted by destroyers, but neither committed battleships. Using battleships at night in the confined waters around the island in the face of a severe torpedo threat was viewed as tactically risky. Despite the fact that the Japanese controlled the waters around the island at night, they were unable to neutralize the airfield, which in turn prevented them from bringing in enough troops and supplies to mount a successful ground offensive to capture the airfield. To solve this dilemma, the IJN mounted what was to be the most successful Japanese battleship action of the war. On October 13, *Kongō* and *Haruna* steamed down "The Slot" at night to conduct a bombardment of the airfield. The two battleships were able to wreak tremendous destruction, with almost 900 14in shells targeting the airfield. This destroyed some 40 aircraft and for the only time on the campaign Henderson Field was briefly neutralized.

The battleship bombardment of Henderson Field allowed most of a Japanese troop convoy to reach Guadalcanal. However, the ensuing Japanese ground attack against the US Marines defending the airfield during October 24–26 failed. This left the Japanese with the same dilemma of getting enough troops to the island for another assault, but not being able to do so until the airfield was neutralized to permit a large troop convoy to reach the island. The solution arrived at was another battleship bombardment – the decisive moment of the entire campaign. If the IJN could successfully neutralize the airfield, enough troops and supplies could be moved to the island for a larger offensive which had a chance of crushing the US Marines garrison. Accordingly, a Japanese task force, including *Hiei* and *Kirishima* and escorted by one light cruiser and 11 destroyers, left the Shortland Islands en route to Guadalcanal. For the first time since the Battle of Cape Esperance on October 11–12, the USN decided to fight the Japanese at night. To thwart the intended bombardment, the USN gathered a force of two heavy cruisers, three light cruisers, and eight destroyers. The resulting battle, fought on the night of November 12/13, was the most vicious and confusing night action of the entire Pacific War. The USN task force was shattered, with two light cruisers sunk, all the other cruisers damaged, and all but two of the destroyers sunk or damaged. In return for these severe losses, the Americans turned back the bombardment force and damaged *Hiei* severely enough that she could not

clear the battle area and was sunk by aircraft the following day. This was the first Japanese battleship lost during the war.

The First Naval Battle of Guadalcanal on November 12–13 did not prove decisive, so the Japanese prepared another battleship bombardment of the airfield as an 11-transport convoy headed for the island. On the night of November 13/14, two Japanese heavy cruisers shelled the airfield but failed to inflict any damage. The next day, aircraft from Henderson Field and the carrier *Enterprise* ravaged the convoy, sinking six transports and damaging another which had to turn back. The remaining four transports were ordered to continue on to Guadalcanal regardless of loss.

Even after the destruction of most of the convoy, the Japanese were determined to neutralize the airfield and get at least a portion of the convoy through. Vice Admiral Kondō Nobutake was charged with executing the operation. He gathered the undamaged *Kirishima*, heavy cruisers *Atago* and *Takao*, and two destroyer squadrons with two light cruisers and nine destroyers and headed south to bombard the airfield during the early-morning hours of November 15. This was a major effort, but could have been mounted in greater strength since *Kongō* and *Haruna*, as well as several heavy cruisers, were north of Guadalcanal but were not committed.

The overall commander of USN forces in the South Pacific, Vice Admiral William "Bull" Halsey, had promised the commander of the US Marines on Guadalcanal that he would use all available forces to support him; but with the surface force committed to stop the first Japanese bombardment shattered, Halsey now had little left to contest this renewed Japanese effort. He assembled his last available ships into a makeshift formation designated Task Force 64. This included the fast battleships *Washington* and *South Dakota* escorted by four destroyers which had never operated together before. This decision risked much since it sent two of the USN's most valuable warships into a tactically unfavorable situation. Designed for a daytime gunnery engagement at long range, the two battleships were being sent into night combat and exposed to a significant torpedo threat. The first battleship duel of the Pacific War was about to unfold.

Hiei was the most modern Kongō-class ship. The Washington Naval Treaty of 1922 required Japan to demilitarize the ship by removing her main armor belt, one of her 14in/45 turrets, and 25 boilers, which reduced her speed to 18kts. This work was completed in 1932, after which *Hiei* served as a training ship. Beginning in 1936, the ship was remilitarized and modernized along the same general lines as the other three ships in the Kongō class, the exception being her superstructure which was of an entirely different design. This view shows *Hiei* in July 1942.

TECHNICAL SPECIFICATIONS

USN BATTLESHIPS

Both ships in the Nevada class, *Nevada* and *Oklahoma*, were laid down in 1912 and commissioned in 1916. As the first USN "superdreadnoughts," they represented the design basis for the next four classes of American battleships.

Nevada-class specifications (1941)	
Units in class	*Nevada*, *Oklahoma*
Displacement	29,065 tons standard; 32,200 tons full load
Dimensions	Length 583ft 7in; beam 107ft 11in; draft 28ft 6in
Maximum speed	20.5kts (*Nevada*); 19.7kts (*Oklahoma*)
Range	8,000nm at 10kts
Protection	Main belt 13.5in; bulkheads 13in; deck 6.5in; turret face 18in; barbette 13in; conning tower 16in
Main and secondary armament	Ten 14in/45; 12 5in/51; eight 5in/25 dual-purpose
Crew	1,374

The two-ship Pennsylvania class was similar to the Nevada class but with incremental firepower enhancements and the fitting of a dedicated underwater protection scheme. *Pennsylvania* was laid down in 1913 and *Arizona* in 1914. Both were commissioned in 1916.

Pennsylvania-class specifications (1941)

Units in class	*Pennsylvania, Arizona*
Displacement	34,823 tons standard; 35,929 tons full load
Dimensions	Length 608ft; beam 106ft 2in; draft 28ft 10in
Maximum speed	21kts
Range	8,000nm at 10kts
Protection	Main belt 13.5in; bulkheads 13in; deck 6.25in; turret face 18in; barbette 13in; conning tower 18in
Main and secondary armament	12 14in/45; 12 5in/51; eight 5in/25 dual-purpose
Crew	1,052

The USN was successful in getting three battleships – the New Mexico class – funded for 1915. All were laid down that year, but the final ship of the class was not commissioned until 1919. Except for the propulsion system on *New Mexico*, these ships were very similar to those of the Pennsylvania class.

New Mexico-class specifications (1941)

Units in class	*New Mexico, Mississippi, Idaho*
Displacement	32,000 tons standard; 33,000 tons full load
Dimensions	Length 624ft; beam 106ft 2in; draft 30ft
Maximum speed	21kts
Range	8,000nm at 10kts
Protection	Main belt 13.5in; bulkheads 13in; deck 8.25in; turret face 18in; barbette 13in; conning tower 18in
Main and secondary armament	12 14in/50; 12 5in/51; eight 5in/25 dual-purpose
Crew	1,084

The two ships of the Tennessee class were commissioned in 1920 and 1921 respectively. They were in most respects a repeat of the New Mexico class but with some refinements to their underwater protection scheme. Both ships were damaged at Pearl Harbor and were rebuilt afterward. The specifications below reflect their new capabilities.

Tennessee-class specifications (as rebuilt)

Units in class	*Tennessee, California*
Displacement	34,858 tons standard; 40,345 tons full load
Dimensions	Length 624ft; beam 114ft; draft 30ft 2in
Maximum speed	20.5kts

Range	8,000nm at 10kts
Protection	Main belt 13.5in; bulkheads 13.5in; deck 3.5in; turret face 18in; barbette 14–16in; conning tower 16in
Main and secondary armament	12 14in/50; 16 5in/38 dual-purpose
Crew	2,375

With the three-ship Colorado class, the USN moved to a 16in/45 main battery. Protection and propulsion were unchanged from the Tennessee class. *Maryland* was commissioned in 1921 and the other two ships were commissioned in 1923. *West Virginia* was rebuilt in a manner identical to the Tennessee class, but she retained her 16in/45 main battery. The other two ships were modernized between the wars, but were not rebuilt during the Pacific War.

Colorado-class specifications (1923)	
Units in class	*Colorado, Maryland, West Virginia*
Displacement	31,800 tons standard; 33,590 tons full load
Dimensions	Length 624ft; beam 97ft 5in; draft 30ft 2in
Maximum speed	21kts
Range	8,000nm at 10kts
Protection	Main belt 13.5in; bulkheads 13.5in; deck 3.5in; turret face 18in; barbette 14–16in; conning tower 16in
Main and secondary armament	Eight 16in/45; 14 5in/51
Crew	1,083

This photograph of *West Virginia* shows her in July 1944 after reconstruction. The ship was entirely modernized, giving her the combat capabilities of a fast battleship. Note the new 5in/38 mounts on the beam. The large radar on the top of the forward superstructure is the SK air-search radar; below it is the cylindrical Mk 8 radar on top of the main-battery fire-control director. A second Mk 34 main-battery director is visible abaft the mainmast.

The USN's first class of fast battleships, the North Carolina class, was laid down in 1937–38, and commissioned in 1941. These ships differed from the "Standard" battleship designs primarily because of their greater speed while retaining the 16in/45 main battery and significant protection.

WEST VIRGINIA

These views depict *West Virginia* in October 1944 at Surigao Strait. The ship has been entirely rebuilt from her pre-Pearl Harbor appearance and now resembles a South Dakota-class battleship. The ship is in a Measure 32/7 dazzle-camouflage scheme. Note the large radar on top of the forward superstructure and the Mk 8 radars on top of the main-battery directors fore and aft.

This is a view of the damage to *North Carolina* when she was torpedoed on September 15, 1942. Note details of antitorpedo protection and the lower edge of the armor belt. The 891lb warhead of the Type 95 torpedo from the IJN submarine *I-19* blew a large hole in the port side of the hull and cracked the armor plate. *North Carolina* was in no danger of sinking, but if sister ship *Washington* had been hit by the larger warhead from a Type 93 torpedo during the Second Naval Battle of Guadalcanal, the damage could have been more severe.

31

North Carolina-class specifications (1941)

Units in class	*North Carolina, Washington*
Displacement	37,484 tons standard; 44,377 tons full load
Dimensions	Length 728ft 9in; beam 108ft 4in; draft 26ft 9in
Maximum speed	28kts
Range	15,000nm at 15kts
Protection	Main belt 12in; bulkheads 11in; deck 5in; turret face 16in; barbette 16in; conning tower 16in
Main and secondary armament	Nine 16in/45; 20 5in/38 dual-purpose
Crew	1,880

The four-ship South Dakota class represented an effort by the USN to emphasize protection. Capabilities were broadly similar to those of the North Carolina class, but additional armor was added while still adhering to the 35,000-ton treaty limit. Three ships were laid down in 1939, and the fourth and final ship in early 1940. All were commissioned in 1942.

South Dakota-class specifications (1942)

Units in class	*South Dakota, Indiana, Massachusetts, Alabama*
Displacement	37,970 tons standard; 44,519 tons full load
Dimensions	Length 680ft; beam 108ft 2in; draft 29ft 3in
Maximum speed	27.5kts
Range	15,000nm at 15kts
Protection	Main belt 12.25in; bulkheads 13.4in; deck 5.3in; turret face 18in; barbette 17.3in; conning tower 15in
Main and secondary armament	Nine 16in/45; 20 (*South Dakota* 16) 5in/38 dual-purpose
Crew	1,793

This photograph from October 26, 1943 shows the silhouette of *New Jersey*. Her profile is dominated by her three 16in/50 turrets and her long bow, the latter a necessary design aspect to meet the requirements for high speed.

These views show *Washington* as she appeared in November 1942 off Guadalcanal. The ship is in a Measure 22 camouflage scheme. Note the large SC radar on the forward superstructure and the Mk 3 radar on top of the main-battery directors fore and aft.

The Iowa class was the result of American battleship designers no longer being restricted by any naval treaty restrictions. The design emphasis was on speed, which was significantly increased thanks to a much more powerful propulsion system and a longer hull. Protection remained similar to that of the preceding South Dakota class. Another modification was the adoption of a more powerful 16in/50 gun.

Iowa-class specifications (1943)	
Units in class	*Iowa*, *New Jersey*, *Missouri*, *Wisconsin*
Displacement	48,110 tons standard; 57,540 tons full load
Dimensions	Length 887ft 3in; beam 108ft 2in; draft 29ft
Maximum speed	32.5kts
Range	15,000nm at 15kts
Protection	Main belt 12.2in; bulkheads 11.2in; deck 5in; turret face 17in; barbette 17.3in; conning tower 17.3in
Main and secondary armament	Nine 16in/50; 20 5in/38 dual-purpose
Crew	1,921

Kirishima anchored off Amoy, China, October 21, 1938 where she was photographed from a USN destroyer. This view clearly shows her two forward 14in/45 twin turrets, the two aft 14in/45 turrets which are trained to starboard, and the seven port-side 6in/50 guns in casemates. Note the main-battery fire-control directors mounted on top of the forward superstructure and on the small superstructure abaft the second stack.

IJN BATTLESHIPS

The oldest class of Japanese battleships to see action during the Pacific War was the Kongō class, laid down between January 1911 and March 1912. The lead ship, *Kongō*, was built in Britain and the following three in Japan. Originally built as battlecruisers, they were modernized between the wars and reclassified as battleships. (The specifications below reflect their battleship specifications.) These ships proved very useful during the war since their high speed made them suitable as carrier escorts and for night-bombardment missions during the Guadalcanal campaign. *Hiei* and *Kirishima* were sunk off Guadalcanal in November 1942. *Kongō* and *Haruna* were active until late in the war, and both fought at Leyte Gulf. *Kongō* was sunk by submarine attack in November 1944 off Taiwan. *Haruna* survived until the end of the war before being sunk at Kure by carrier air raids in July 1945.

Kongō-class specifications (1941)	
Units in class	*Kongō, Hiei, Haruna, Kirishima*
Displacement	32,056 tons standard; 36,601 tons full load
Dimensions	Length 738ft 7in; beam 95ft 3in; draft 32ft
Maximum speed	30.5kts
Range	10,000nm at 18kts
Protection	Main belt 8in; bulkheads 8in; deck 4.75in; turret face 9in; barbette 10in; conning tower 10in
Main and secondary armament	Eight 14in/45; 14 6in/50; eight 5in/40 dual-purpose
Crew	1,221

The first IJN superdreadnoughts, the Fusō class, were laid down in 1912 and 1913. *Fusō* was commissioned in 1915 and *Yamashiro* in 1917. The intent to build a battleship superior to any foreign rival was successful in regards to firepower and speed, but the two ships of this class were deficient in protection.

KIRISHIMA

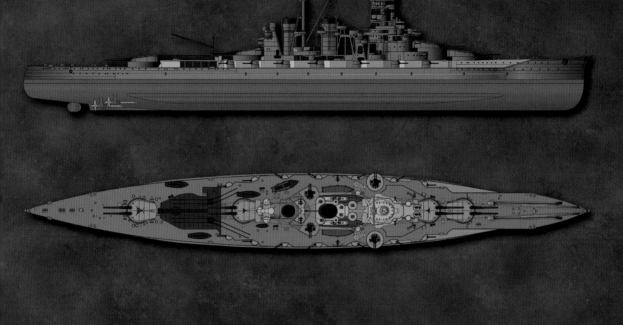

Kirishima is depicted in these views as she appeared in November 1942 when she was sunk. The ship's pre-World War I origin is obvious given the antiquated arrangement of her 14in/45 turrets and the casemate-mounted secondary battery. The large forward superstructure was added during modernizations between the wars. Note the ship carries no radar.

Yamashiro and Fusō photographed after both had undergone modernization. Despite the extensive work put into both, they remained second-line units by virtue of their slow speed and weak protection. There are several ways to tell these sister ships apart. Yamashiro in the foreground has a better-balanced pagoda superstructure (unlike that of Fusō in the background); Yamashiro's Number 3 14in/45 turret faced aft (Fusō's faced forward); Yamashiro had her aircraft-handling facilities on the stern, while Fusō's were on her Number 3 turret.

Fusō-class specifications (1941)

Units in class	*Fusō, Yamashiro*
Displacement	34,700 tons standard; 39,154 tons full load
Dimensions	Length 698ft; beam 100ft 6in; draft 31ft 9in
Maximum speed	24.75kts
Range	8,000nm at 14kts
Protection	Main belt 12in; bulkheads 12in; deck 5.1in; turret face 12in; barbette 8–12in; conning tower 13.75in
Main and secondary armament	12 14in/45; 14 6in/50; eight 5in/40 dual-purpose
Crew	1,400

The two-ship Ise class, laid down in 1915, was essentially a repeat of the Fusō class with minimal improvements in protection and a modified main-battery arrangement. By the start of the Pacific War, both were considered to be second-line units and consequently saw little action. They were selected for conversion into hybrid battleship-carriers, but conducted only one operation in this configuration. The impracticality of the entire scheme was highlighted by the fact that on this occasion they carried no aircraft. Both were sunk by USN carrier aircraft bombs in July 1945 near Kure.

Ise-class specifications (1941)

Units in class	*Ise, Hyūga*
Displacement	35,800 tons standard; 40,169 tons full load
Dimensions	Length 708ft; beam 104ft; draft 30ft
Maximum speed	25.3kts
Range	9,500nm at 16kts
Protection	Main belt 12in; bulkheads 12in; deck 4.7in; turret face 12in; barbette 12in; conning tower 14in
Main and secondary armament	12 14in/45; 16 5.5in/50; eight 5in/40 dual-purpose
Crew	1,360

This view of *Hyūga* was taken at Amoy, China in December 1936 from a Royal Navy light cruiser. It shows the primary difference from the preceding Fusō class – both midships 14in/45 turrets have been placed together abaft the stack.

YAMASHIRO

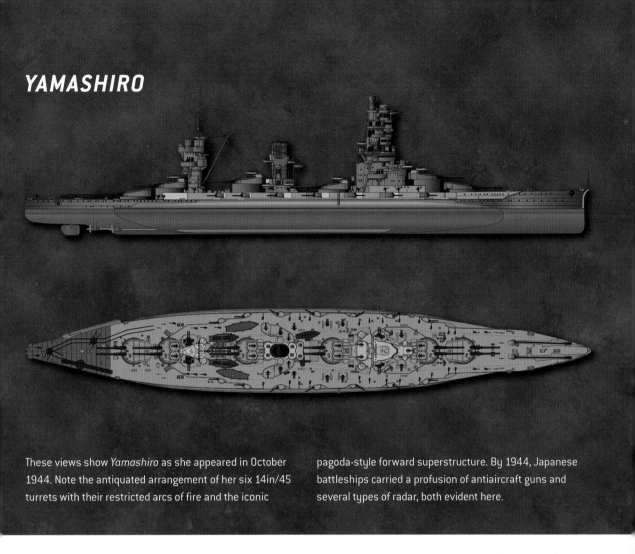

These views show *Yamashiro* as she appeared in October 1944. Note the antiquated arrangement of her six 14in/45 turrets with their restricted arcs of fire and the iconic pagoda-style forward superstructure. By 1944, Japanese battleships carried a profusion of antiaircraft guns and several types of radar, both evident here.

The IJN's first battleship fitted with 16.1in/45 guns was *Nagato*. Laid down in 1917, she was commissioned in 1920. The second ship of the Nagato class, *Mutsu*, was begun in 1918 and escaped the terms of the Washington Naval Treaty to be commissioned in 1921. *Nagato* was the only IJN battleship to survive the Pacific War still afloat. *Mutsu* was destroyed by a magazine explosion in June 1943.

Nagato-class specifications (1941)	
Units in class	*Nagato*, *Mutsu*
Displacement	39,130 tons standard; 46,356 tons full load
Dimensions	Length 734ft; beam 108ft; draft 31ft
Maximum speed	25kts
Range	8,560nm at 16kts
Protection	Main belt 12in; bulkheads 12in; deck 8.1in; turret face 18.1in; barbette 12in; conning tower 14.6in
Main and secondary armament	Eight 16.1in/45; 18 5.5in/50; eight 5in/40 dual-purpose
Crew	1,368

This photograph of *Mutsu* shows her in her post-modernization configuration. Note the four 16.1in/45 twin turrets and the 5.5in/50 guns in casemates. *Nagato* and *Mutsu* represented the IJN's counterpart to the USN's Colorado class.

The ultimate expression of the IJN's desire to gain a qualitative edge over the USN was the Yamato class. With its 18.1in/45 main battery, the firepower of this class looked to be unsurpassed; in reality the 18.1in/45 gun was inaccurate and the USN's 16in/50 gun on the Iowa class was superior ballistically. The scale of protection of the Yamato class was also unsurpassed, but its underwater protection scheme was flawed. The lead ship, *Yamato*, was laid down in 1937 and commissioned within days of the Pearl Harbor attack, which demonstrated that the day of the battleship had passed. Construction of *Musashi* was begun in 1938 and she joined the fleet in mid-1942. The third ship of the class, *Shinano*, was completed as an aircraft carrier, but was sunk on her maiden voyage in November 1944 by submarine attack. Work on a modified fourth ship was halted in 1941.

Yamato-class specifications (1941)

Units in class	*Yamato, Musashi*
Displacement	62,315 tons standard; 69,998 tons full load
Dimensions	Length 862ft; beam 121ft; draft 35ft 6in
Maximum speed	27.5kts
Range	7,200nm at 16kts
Protection	Main belt 16in; bulkheads 11.8in; deck 9.1in; turret face 26in; barbette 21.5–16in; conning tower 19.7in
Main and secondary armament	Nine 18.1in/45; 12 6.1in/60; 12 5in/40 dual-purpose
Crew	2,300

USN BATTLESHIP GUNS

The entire purpose of a battleship is acting as a well-protected platform for large-caliber guns. The larger the gun, the larger the shell which contributes to its penetrative power. More important for determining penetration capabilities was the velocity of the shell. The longer the gun, the higher the velocity; the higher the velocity, the greater the penetration. In general, the USN favored a lighter, faster shell over a heavier, slower shell. The down side of a high-velocity weapon is that it increases barrel wear.

Alabama on her shakedown cruise in December 1942. The ship is wearing a striking Measure 12 (modified) camouflage scheme. The shorter hull compared to the preceding North Carolina class allowed a greater level of protection over a shorter expanse of hull. Note the Mk 8 fire-control radars on the two main-battery directors.

USN battleship main and secondary guns				
Type	Shell weight	Muzzle velocity	Maximum range	Rate of fire
Main guns				
14in/45 (Nevada and Pennsylvania classes)	1,500lb	2,600ft/sec	34,300yd	1–2rd/min
14in/50 (New Mexico and Tennessee classes)	1,500lb	2,700ft/sec	36,600yd	1–2rd/min
16in/45 (Colorado class)	2,240lb	2,520ft/sec	35,000yd	1–2rd/min
16in/45 (North Carolina and South Dakota classes)	2,700lb	2,300ft/sec	36,900yd	2rd/min
16in/50 (Iowa class)	2,700lb	2,500ft/sec	42,345yd	2rd/min
Secondary guns				
5in/51	50lb	3,150ft/sec	15,850yd	8–9rd/min
5in/25	54lb	2,110ft/sec	14,500yd	14rd/min
5in/38	55lb	2,600ft/sec	18,200yd	15–20rd/min

USN WEAPONRY

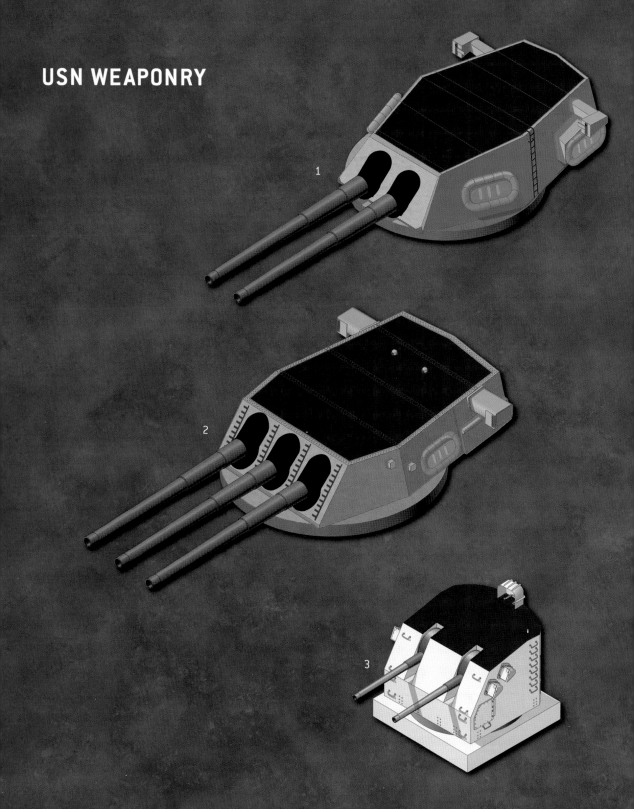

Three USN battleship weapons are depicted in this plate: a 16in/45 twin turret (**1**) of the type found on *West Virginia*; a 16in/45 triple turret (**2**) of the type found on *South Dakota*; and a 5in/38 dual mount (**3**) of the type found on all modern USN battleships and most of the older battleships which were rebuilt or modernized during the Pacific War.

IJN WEAPONRY

Three IJN battleship weapons are depicted in this plate: a 14in/45 twin turret with rangefinder (**1**); a 14in/45 twin turret without rangefinder (**2**); and a 6in/50 casemated gun (**3**) of the type found on the Kongō and Fusō classes. (Artworks on pages 40 and 41 are not shown to scale.)

This is *Musashi* leaving Brunei Bay on October 22, 1944, en route to a planned attack on the USN invasion fleet in Leyte Gulf. This view shows her majestic profile with a large superstructure, stack, and three immense turrets for her 18.1in/45 guns. *Musashi* was sunk two days later in the Sibuyan Sea having never fired her main battery at an American surface target during the war, testimony to the futility of even the largest battleships ever built operating in the face of naval air power.

OPPOSITE

These are the forward 16.1in/45 turrets aboard *Nagato*. Each turret was heavily armored with 18.1in face, 11in side, 7.5in rear, and 9.8–9.0in roof armor. The IJN's 16.1in/45 gun fired a 2,249lb armor-piercing or 2,064lb high-explosive shell. Later in the war, a special shrapnel shell was introduced for antiaircraft fire.

IJN BATTLESHIP GUNS

Eight of the 12 IJN battleships carried a main battery of 14in/45 guns; the gun was based on a British design. The 16.1in/45 guns aboard the Nagato class were Japanese-designed; the Yamato class carried the unsurpassed 18.1in/45 gun. Secondary batteries on IJN battleships were intended primarily to counter torpedo attack by destroyers. The 6in/50 gun on the Kongō and Fusō classes was based on a British design, but on these ships the secondary battery was placed in casemates which reduced its arc of fire. The Ise and Nagato classes were fitted with the Japanese-designed 5.5in/50 gun. These were still fitted in casemates, but enjoyed a better location. The secondary battery of the Yamato class consisted of four 6.1in/50 triple turrets originally fitted on Mogami-class heavy cruisers.

IJN battleship main and secondary guns				
Type	Shell weight	Muzzle velocity	Maximum range	Rate of fire
Main guns				
14in/45 41st Year Type (1908)	1,485lb	2,543ft/sec	38,770yd	1–2rd/min
16.1in/45 3rd Year Type (1914)	2,249lb	2,575ft/sec	42,000yd	2rd/min
18.1in/45 Type 94	3,219lb	2,575ft/sec	45,960yd	2rd/min
Secondary guns				
5.5in/50 3rd Year Type (1914)	84lb	2,805ft/sec	21,600yd	6rd/min
6in/50 41st Year Type (1908)	100lb	2,805ft/sec	22,970yd	4–6rd/min
6.1in/60 3rd Year Type (1914)	123lb	3,035ft/sec	29,960yd	5rd/min

USN FIRE-CONTROL SYSTEMS

Since the key to any gunnery engagement at sea is effective fire control, each navy's fire-control system is briefly discussed here. USN doctrine demanded that its battleships use their main batteries at long ranges to deal crippling blows to an opposing battle fleet. Long-range engagements were especially stressing to fire-control systems and tactics. To hit an enemy ship at any range, the range of the target, its movement, and the firing ship's own movement had to be calculated and continually updated. This necessitated a complex fire-control system.

The basis for long-range fire was a rangefinder to determine the range to the target, and every USN battleship carried several of these. USN battleship cage masts or superstructures contained fire-control directors and facilities for spotting the fall of the ship's shells. The center of USN battleship fire control was the main-battery plot. This was located below decks and was protected by the ship's armor. It contained an analog computer which calculated the fire-control solution using inputs from other parts of the fire-control system. Eventually, the fast battleships, as well as the rebuilt *Tennessee*, *California*, and *West Virginia*, were equipped with automatic control which moved the main-battery turrets in accordance with directions from the main-battery plot by means of elevation and training drives in the turrets. This allowed a constant aim to be maintained. Effective gunnery required the observation of the fall of the ship's shells so the required corrections could be made. This was done by observers on the tallest part of the ship or, if available, by the ship's spotting aircraft. The most effective method to determine range and the fall of shot was by radar. As the war progressed, the USN replaced rangefinders with radar. The incorporation of radar into its fire-control system gave the Americans a huge advantage over the IJN.

This prewar view of *Colorado* shows her cage masts and secondary battery in casemates. Note the presence of three spotting aircraft, which were an important component of her fire-control system at the time. The requirement to spot the fall of shot was taken over by radar during the war.

The greatest difference between USN and IJN fire-control tactics was the heavy American reliance on radar. The introduction of radar was a revolution in fire control, and the previous forms of spotting fire were abandoned. The standard tactic of "laddering" – firing for effect by changing the range up and down by 200yd across the target – was also abandoned. The advent of radar meant that fire was now opened at the measured range. In effect, radar was serving as a much faster and more accurate rangefinder.

The first important gunnery radar mounted on USN battleships was the Mk 3 set which began to reach service in 1941. This provided a range on a large ship from 15,000yd to 30,000yd. The Mk 3 possessed only a limited beam definition, however, which meant that the targets could be confused for the splashes of shells. The Mk 3 was therefore susceptible to operator confusion, which led to the target escaping with the splashes being engaged instead. This shortcoming was worst when engaging a high-speed target (such as a destroyer) which could quickly pass out of the range gate set around the target by the radar operator, and when a high rate of fire created a large number of splashes.

The much more effective Mk 8 radar began to reach the fleet in 1943. This radar was fitted on the Mk 38 director on the USN's modern battleships and a select few of the modernized older battleships. The biggest improvement was that the S-band Mk 8 provided errors in direction, something the Mk 3 with its broad beams could not. Because the system could lock onto the target and search for the splashes, there was no need for the other methods of spotting fire. This translated into a system capable of blind fire, which obviously was an immense advantage in night combat – the conditions in which the Pacific War battleship actions were fought. The Mk 8 could track a battleship-sized target at 40,000yd and up to 31,000yd on a smaller target, giving American battleships a potentially considerable range advantage.

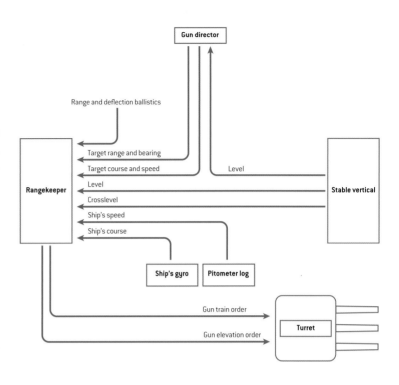

The fire-control system on USN battleships was complex. This schematic shows the principal elements of that system.

IJN FIRE-CONTROL SYSTEMS

In general, IJN fire-control systems lagged behind those of the USN. Once the USN integrated radar into its fire-control doctrine, the edge enjoyed by the USN increased. This difference was most marked at night when low visibility hindered the ability of

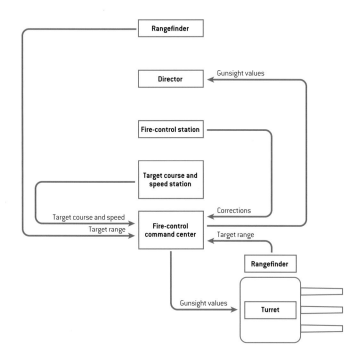

```
Rangefinder

Director ←——— Gunsight values

Fire-control station

Target course and
speed station

                      ←——— Corrections
Target course and speed
Target range            Fire-control
                        command center    Target range ———→

                                          Rangefinder

                        Gunsight values ———→   Turret
```

IJN battleship fire-control systems were generally similar to those found on their USN counterparts, but were less modern and overall, less capable. This schematic shows the principal elements of the IJN system.

conventional optics to measure the distance to, and the course and speed of, the target. Since both battleship clashes during the Pacific War between the USN and IJN occurred at night, the fire-control capabilities of the respective navies were probably the most important factor in determining the winner.

Japanese battleship fire-control capabilities benefited greatly from the IJN's World War I-era alliance with Britain's Royal Navy. Early Japanese fire-control equipment was based on British designs; and as late as 1925, the Japanese received fire-control equipment from the British. Standard fire-control equipment on IJN battleships included the Type 92 table (an early fire-control computer) which depended on manual inputs and was fairly slow in generating a target solution. Feeding the Type 92 was a course- and speed-measurement device which was uniquely Japanese. Rangefinders were mounted as high up as possible in the ship's superstructure; Japanese rangefinders were of the coincidence type and were of high quality. The main-battery director was also mounted high up on the superstructure. Beginning in 1942, three types of radar were fitted on IJN battleships. One was designed for surface search and had a theoretical detection range against a battleship-sized target of up to 13nm, but no IJN radar had the power and accuracy to be truly effective as gunnery radar.

IJN doctrine called for long-range fire and battleships trained extensively to shoot at extended ranges. The Japanese planned to track enemy targets at maximum tracking range – 43,745yd – and open fire at 37,185yd. By doing so, they calculated that they had a 4,375–5,470yd advantage over USN battleships. IJN battleships fired half-salvos when ranging the target; once the target was straddled, full broadsides were used.

Since the two actions being examined in this book were both fought at night, Japanese night-fighting tactics and equipment should be reviewed. Night fighting was an integral part of the IJN's prewar planning for a decisive battle, so much thought and effort was expended in developing the necessary tactics and equipment. The specialized night-fighting equipment was world-class. Star shells, including a variant suspended by parachute, flares dropped by floatplanes, and smokeless powder were all available. Japanese expertise in optics was evidenced by the 8.3in-diameter night-vision binoculars which in the early part of the war proved superior in some cases to early USN radars. The IJN's attention to night fighting paid large dividends early in the war, but by 1943 any edge enjoyed by the IJN at night had been negated by USN radar.

THE COMBATANTS

USN BATTLESHIP TACTICS

The USN expected to have a numerical advantage in battleships over the IJN. To bring this advantage to bear, the USN gave considerable thought and devoted much practice to the pre-gunnery phases of a fleet action. Determining the enemy's exact location was crucial for the proper employment of the battle line. Up until 1939, scouting was the primary responsibility for cruisers. After that point, it was recognized that aircraft could perform this function better while reducing the vulnerability of cruisers to enemy action.

Once the enemy was located, the approach phase was initiated. This could take several days and came to be dominated by naval air power. In a series of annual fleet exercises, called Fleet Problems, carriers demonstrated that they were essential for scouting and gaining the air superiority necessary to allow aircraft to be used for spotting friendly gunfire. However, even though aircraft carriers were shown to be vulnerable to each other, they seemed unable to stop the advance of the main battle fleet. This placed the battleship in the role of being the only ship which could successfully engage another battleship.

Following the approach phase, the engagement phase began. Each division of three battleships steamed in parallel lines. This formation permitted a quick turn in either direction to form a single line which would bring its broadside to bear on the enemy. At the crucial moment, the deployment of the battle line would be ordered and quick and accurate gunfire brought to bear on the enemy's battleships.

The engagement phase focused on the destruction of the Japanese battle line. USN battleships were trained to conduct long-range fire and to concentrate fire on their Japanese counterparts as quickly as possible. Even with the best fire-control system in the world, however, the USN found conducting accurate long-range gunnery to be

North Carolina, photographed in April 1942. The first class of modern USN battleships was equipped with three 16in/45 triple turrets and ten 5in/38 twin mounts.

extremely difficult. A well-trained crew could direct fire on a target at ranges of over 30,000yd. In the series of Fleet Problems, opening engagement ranges gradually increased to 35,000yd. Once a fire-control solution was gained, the USN emphasized full eight- or 12-gun salvos. Spotters on the tops of the battleship masts were challenged to spot fire since at 30,000yd only the superstructure of an enemy battleship was visible because of the curvature of the earth at that range. Even well-trained gun crews and observers saw their accuracy significantly decrease at long range. This tendency could be mitigated by using aircraft for spotting. A Naval War College estimate stated that spotting with aircraft would result in six times more hits.

Comparing the equipment and tactics of the prewar USN with those of the IJN, neither side possessed a marked advantage in gunnery accuracy. A hypothetical large-scale gunnery duel would have been more heavily influenced by the greater numbers of USN battleships and their generally higher level of side and horizontal protection. An even greater influence on the battle lines would have been the impact of naval air power in which both sides were at rough parity. Both navies expected their carrier forces to neutralize the enemy's; had one side gained an advantage, this would have been a significant factor in the gunnery phase. Another potential factor was the superiority of the IJN's torpedoes which possessed a range comparable to that of USN battleship guns. The Americans were entirely ignorant of this development, which could have had devastating consequences.

IJN BATTLESHIP TACTICS

The IJN developed an intricate set of tactics for the expected decisive battleship clash with the USN, but to say that these were unrealistic would be an understatement. During the war, there was never the remotest chance that they would be brought into action.

Like the USN, the Japanese still placed the battleship at the center of any decisive battle. This was affirmed by the Battle Instructions of 1934 which stated: "The battleship divisions are the main weapon in a fleet battle and their task is to engage the main force of the enemy." Other fleet elements had a role in this battle, but only the battleships could deliver the final, crushing blow. In general terms, this is how the IJN saw a battleship duel as unfolding. The vanguard force would be built around the four Kongō-class fast battleships, while the main battle force consisted of the IJN's other six battleships broken down into three divisions of two ships each. After air superiority had been gained by the carriers, the battle force would gain a position roughly parallel to the USN battle line at a range of 43,600yd. The Kongō-class vessels would support the destroyers and cruisers of the vanguard force which would launch a massive torpedo attack on the American battle line before the gunnery phase. Following the chaos arising from the torpedo attack, the IJN battle line would close

WILLIS A. LEE, JR.

A distant relative of the famous Robert E. Lee of Civil War fame, Lee graduated from the United States Naval Academy at Annapolis, Maryland in 1908. His early career was marked by several tours of duty with the Academy rifle team; he set a record by winning seven medals at the 1920 Olympics in Antwerp. He went on to be recognized as the USN's foremost expert on battleship gunnery and was instrumental in introducing radar into fire control.

Soon after the United States entered World War II, Lee was promoted to rear admiral and assigned as Assistant Chief of Staff to the Commander in Chief, US Fleet. Lee got a chance to put his knowledge of gunnery to use in August 1942 when he assumed command of Battleship Division Six, consisting of the new battleships *Washington* and *South Dakota*. Lee commanded Task Force 64 centered around *Washington* which was positioned south of Guadalcanal in October 1942 to counter any major Japanese move against the island. On the night of November 14/15, the battleships were committed to surface combat. Lee turned a risky situation around and gained a major victory through his knowledge and effective use of radar which allowed him to shoot and maneuver skillfully. With *South Dakota* knocked out of the battle early, he maneuvered his flagship *Washington* to surprise and sink *Kirishima*, turning a potentially reckless gamble into a decisive victory. Lee himself was under no illusions when he described his victory: "We realized then and it should not be forgotten now, that our entire superiority was due almost entirely to our possession of radar. Certainly we have no edge on the Japs in experience, skill, training, or performance of personnel."

Lee went on to command the Pacific Fleet's battleships. They were tethered to the Fast Carrier Task Force for the remainder of the war where they proved useful as antiaircraft platforms. In May 1945, Lee was ordered to form a special unit to engineer ways to combat the menace posed by *kamikaze* aerial attack. While serving in this capacity, he suffered a heart attack and died on August 25, 1945.

THOMAS C. KINKAID

Graduating from the United States Naval Academy in 1908, Kinkaid became an ordnance expert with an emphasis on fire-control systems. After serving aboard the battleship *Arizona* in World War I, he received his first command, of a destroyer, in 1924. His second command was the heavy cruiser *Indianapolis* in 1937. Immediately after the Pacific War began, Kinkaid assumed command of a cruiser division in the Pacific Fleet, seeing action at Coral Sea and Midway. He began the Guadalcanal campaign as commander of Task Force 16, but the carrier *Enterprise* was damaged at Eastern Solomons in August 1942 and forced to return to Pearl Harbor for repairs. Kinkaid, a non-aviator, commanded two carrier task forces at the Battle of Santa Cruz in October 1942; the battle was a major USN defeat, with the carrier *Hornet* being sunk and *Enterprise* damaged again.

In January 1943, Kinkaid became Commander of the North Pacific Force and was ordered to get along with the US Army commands in the area. Kinkaid directed the recapture of Attu and Kiska in the Aleutians and showed that he was able to work within a complex command structure with Army generals. This made him a natural fit for his next job — Commander, Allied Naval Forces Southwest Pacific Area and Commander of the 7th Fleet. In the series of naval encounters known collectively as the Battle of Leyte Gulf, Kinkaid's 7th Fleet fought at Surigao Strait and off Samar Island. At Surigao Strait, Kinkaid and his on-scene commander fought a near-perfect battle against an outnumbered Japanese force. This was offset by the Battle of Samar during which a large Japanese surface force surprised a group of escort carriers. Though the battle resulted in an American victory, the price was high. The commander of the neighboring 3rd Fleet, Vice Admiral William "Bull" Halsey, is usually blamed for the fact that the escort carriers were exposed to attack, but Kinkaid shared some of this responsibility. Kinkaid was promoted to full admiral in April 1945 and the 7th Fleet ended the war with a series of amphibious operations on Borneo. Kinkaid retired in 1950 and died in 1972.

to some 38,000yd and begin to engage using the 16.1in/45 guns on *Nagato* and *Mutsu*. The effect of the torpedoes and long-range battleship gunnery was expected to be devastating. Once this was realized, the Japanese battleships would close to 20,700–24,000yd and finish off the Americans.

The basic doctrine underpinning the IJN's decisive battle strategy was to outrange the enemy. This doctrine first applied to the big guns of the battleships, but eventually reached every part of the fleet, from ships carrying torpedoes to submarines and naval aircraft. To allow the battleships to engage at the longest possible range, the fire-control systems of the battleships were upgraded. The IJN undertook a marked modernization of its fire-control capabilities in the period from 1926 until the beginning of the war, but overall the Japanese fell behind the USN in terms of fire-control instrumentation. The basis for long-range fire by the IJN was provided by their excellent rangefinder optics. The information from these devices was used to best advantage by virtue of intensive training. In 1939, the Japanese reported 12 percent accuracy at 35,000yd, but this claim seems doubtful since it was never achieved by any navy at any point during the war. In the early part of the conflict, IJN gunnery proved as accurate as USN gunnery, but this changed as soon as the USN began to incorporate and rely upon radar to control gunnery.

Another tactic to increase range and accuracy was the use of spotter aircraft launched from the battleships. Using aircraft also permitted the Japanese to employ smokescreens to hide their own ships from observation. This tactic was mastered by 1935 and afterward became a staple for the planned decisive gunnery duel. By using all these measures, the Japanese reckoned they possessed a tactically significant range advantage over the American battle fleet of 4,360–5,450yd.

At the heart of the IJN's battle line before the Pacific War were *Nagato* and *Mutsu*, the IJN's only battleships carrying 16.1in/45 guns. This is a view of *Nagato* participating in gunnery exercises in May 1936 after the completion of her interwar modernization. During the war, *Nagato* contributed little, but was the only surviving IJN battleship at the time of Japan's surrender. Sister ship *Mutsu* was sunk by an unexplained magazine explosion in June 1943.

USN TRAINING

Since USN battleships were expected to punish their IJN counterparts at long range, they focused on long-range gunnery under daylight conditions. The dominant view in the USN was that gunnery was the key to victory. This led to a focus on the Navy's ultimate gunnery platform, its battleships, but also translated into a concentration on gunnery for cruisers and destroyers.

Concentration on battleship gunnery was out of place in the actual battle conditions prevailing in November 1942 around Guadalcanal. All surface battles were fought at night since the Japanese could not approach the island with its airfield during daylight. USN night doctrine did not see a role for battleships in a night engagement other than as an asset to be protected for the inevitable daylight battle in which its long-range guns could be employed to full effect. It would be incorrect to contend that the USN did not train for night combat, but the problem was that this training focused on what was called "Major Tactics" which were associated with the decisive engagement

between battle lines. In some respects, this night-fighting training was like that practiced by the Japanese. American cruisers and destroyers exercised locating and attacking Japanese battleships at close range with torpedoes. The training to attack a slow-moving and usually illuminated battleship came at the expense of "Minor Tactics" which dealt with combat between light units.

At Guadalcanal, Rear Admiral Willis A. Lee, Jr., had to devise tactics for his battleships on the fly since prewar doctrine did not apply. In general, the introduction of radar meant that he could easily employ his 16in guns at night at ranges of 10,000yd or more. This meant that Japanese destroyers or cruisers could be engaged before they got within effective torpedo range. At this point in the war, the Americans still had not processed the true capabilities of the IJN's Type 93 torpedo.

On top of the handicap that Lee faced of having no reliable night-fighting doctrine, he faced the Japanese with a totally improvised force. Ships and commanders that have spent time working together on an extended basis can overcome a lack of doctrine. At the Second Naval Battle of Guadalcanal, however, Task Force 64 was hastily thrown together. All four destroyers were from different divisions and had never worked together. Likewise, *Washington* and *South Dakota* had never had a chance to work together. On the positive side, both battleships had ample time to work up when commissioned, and both had well-trained crews. *South Dakota* had already seen action at the Battle of Santa Cruz in October 1942, when Captain Thomas Gatch's well-drilled antiaircraft crews played a major role in the battle protecting the carrier *Enterprise* from air attack. Observers stated that Gatch's ship was dirty, but his gunners were top notch. *Washington* had not seen action yet, but Lee selected her as his flagship. Lee was a pioneer in the integration of radar into gunnery control.

Going into 1944, the USN had proven its ability to adapt to the changing nature of naval warfare. After an uncertain start, the USN had revamped its night-fighting doctrine which was now built around the incorporation of radar. The key difference was the utilization of the full offensive potential of destroyers. They were now unleashed to use radar to help execute independent torpedo attacks on Japanese ships. This tactic proved deadly during the later part of the Solomons campaign in 1943 when the Americans eclipsed the night-fighting superiority of the Japanese. Another major enhancement was the employment of cruiser guns at night controlled by radar. The fast-firing light cruisers were especially suited for this since their high rate of fire could literally flood a target under a barrage of shells.

IJN TRAINING

The prewar IJN stressed realistic and arduous training – an essential building block if the Japanese were to make up for their numerical inferiority compared to the USN. The IJN was an offensive force, and speed, firepower, and finely honed crews fit that model perfectly. Night training was a focus area; proficiency in night action was crucial since it was required to attrite the American battle line before the climactic gunnery duel. This would be accomplished by Japanese destroyers and heavy cruisers attacking USN battleships with gunfire and torpedoes. Eventually, the Kongō-class battleships were given a role in night combat since their high speed allowed them to support the heavy cruisers and destroyers. By the time of the Guadalcanal campaign, the IJN was the best-trained night-fighting navy in the world and the high prewar standards of training were still much in evidence.

By 1944, the quality of IJN personnel and training was waning in the face of wartime losses and expansion. This was mitigated by the IJN's propensity to keep personnel assigned to the same ship for long periods, and all of the Japanese ships present at Surigao Strait in October 1944 were in commission before December 1941. Nevertheless, the force given to Vice Admiral Nishimura Shōji was decidedly second string. The two battleships were the oldest and slowest in the fleet and had seen little action during the war. *Fusō* at least spent much of 1943 and 1944 in the forward area, operating out of Truk Atoll with the Combined Fleet. She saw no action, however, and her time at Truk was not spent training but in constant readiness. *Yamashiro* was even less active. With the exception of a single ferry mission to Truk in October–November 1943 carrying Army troops, she remained in the Inland Sea. In September 1943, she was designated as a training ship for midshipmen. Not until September 1944 was *Yamashiro* brought back to front-line status. The rest of Nishimura's force was also second-rate. *Mogami* was converted into an aircraft-carrying cruiser in 1943, and had lost two of her 8in turrets in the process. His four destroyers were Shiratsuyu- and Asahio-class ships, the oldest assigned to the First Diversion Attack Force. None of these ships had worked together, and their commanding officers were unfamiliar to each other.

Hiei was demilitarized in accordance with the terms of the Washington Naval Treaty which limited the IJN's total tonnage in battleships. This is *Hiei* pictured during her period as a training ship; note the absence of the aft 14in/45 turret. She was modernized and brought back into service before the start of the Pacific War, but no amount of modernization could make a battlecruiser designed before 1911 competitive with modern USN battleships.

KONDŌ NOBUTAKE

Kondō graduated from the IJN's naval academy at Etajima in 1907 first among 172 cadets. After attending the Naval Staff College, he returned as an instructor before assuming command of the heavy cruiser *Kako* in 1929 and the battleship *Kongō* in 1932. He assumed flag rank in November 1933 and was promoted to vice admiral in November 1937. A prominent member of the battleship clique, Kondō was assigned roles of increasing responsibility including Chief of Staff of the Combined Fleet in 1935 followed by head of the Operations Staff on the Naval General Staff (December 1935–December 1938). He also held important sea-going commands, and at the start of the Pacific War he commanded the 2nd Fleet, providing the majority of the heavy forces for the invasions of the Philippines, Malaya, and the Dutch East Indies, meaning Kondō had overall command of these operations which were crucial for Japan's success in the war.

Kondō then led the Midway Invasion Force during the IJN's unsuccessful attack on the island in June 1942, and commanded the Advance Force in the carrier battles of Eastern Solomons (August 1942) and Santa Cruz (October 1942) during the Guadalcanal campaign. During the decisive clashes in November 1942, Kondō was unable to neutralize the American airfield by way of a battleship bombardment. After the first failed attempt which cost the IJN its first battleship of the war, Kondō personally led the second attempt on the night of November 14/15. He was surprised by two modern American battleships which defeated his bombardment operation, sinking the battleship *Kirishima* in the process. Kondō failed to press home the advantage gained early in the battle, and was the loser in what could be considered a reckless venture by the USN to risk two battleships at night in the torpedo-infested waters of Iron Bottom Sound. His failure brought an end to his sea-going career. He was retained as Deputy Commander of the Combined Fleet and later promoted to full admiral in April 1943. In December 1943, he assumed command of the China Area Fleet and held this post until May 1945. He died at age 66 in 1953.

NISHIMURA SHŌJI

Graduating from the IJN's naval academy in 1911, Nishimura started as a navigation expert, but later switched to torpedoes. At 27, he gained his first command, a destroyer. Known as a "sea dog" who detested time spent ashore, Nishimura later commanded a destroyer division and a heavy cruiser. He attended the Naval Staff College during 1936–38, but was allowed to take the Naval Staff College exams without completing all the classes.

In November 1941, Nishimura gained flag rank and took command of Destroyer Squadron 4. However, his checkered war record, combined with personal tragedy when his only son was killed on December 23, 1941 in a flying accident in the Philippines, appeared to give him a fatalistic attitude. Always aggressive, he was not held responsible for a series of misfortunes suffered by forces under his command. The largest misstep was at the Battle of Balikpapan in February 1942 when the convoy he was escorting was attacked by USN destroyers with impunity. In July 1942, Nishimura was given command of a squadron of heavy cruisers which conducted the ineffectual bombardment of Henderson Field on Guadalcanal on the night of November 14/15. In spite of this, in November 1943 he was promoted to vice admiral.

After a short period ashore, Nishimura was assigned to take over Battleship Division 2 in September 1944 and ordered to take part in the decisive battle for Leyte the following month. There was a definite sacrificial element to Nishimura's role at Leyte. His two elderly battleships were seen as expendable; detached from the main body of the fleet because of their low speed, they were probably viewed as decoys by all concerned. This, and Nishimura's personal attitude, added up to a doomed operation at Leyte in which all but one of his seven ships were destroyed. Even in view of his disastrous defeat at Surigao Strait in October 1944, however, Nishimura was not the rash fool he is most often made out to be. By all accounts from both subordinates and superiors, he was a serious and studious man who considered all options during planning. During execution, he was determined and undoubtedly brave.

COMBAT

BATTLESHIP DUEL OFF GUADALCANAL

The campaign for Guadalcanal included the longest naval campaign of the Pacific War. Not unexpectedly, this included the initial clash of battleships in the Pacific between the USN and IJN. By November 1942, with the campaign coming to a decisive point, both the Americans and Japanese were forced to employ battleships. The first clash of battleships took place on the night of November 14/15 at the Second Naval Battle of Guadalcanal. The USN commander, Rear Admiral Willis Lee, expected to be outnumbered, but was unsure of the precise composition of the Japanese force bearing down on Guadalcanal. The IJN commander, Vice Admiral Kondō Nobutake, also expected to encounter opposition in the course of conducting his bombardment mission, but had no idea he was about to run into two modern battleships.

Both sides expected contact with the enemy and both commanders made allowance for it. Kondō had received reports of three USN forces active on November 14 off Guadalcanal. The presence of two battleships was indicated in one of these reports, but at 2230hrs on November 14 he received a report from *Kirishima*'s floatplane that two cruisers and four destroyers were 50nm to his south. In Kondō's mind, this confirmed the usual American pattern of withdrawing their battleships to escort the carrier operating southeast of Guadalcanal. In any event, it was clear that a night engagement was in the offing. He took to heart the lessons of the night action of November 12/13 when the first IJN bombardment force was surprised by an American cruiser–destroyer force. This time he planned to send two groups of destroyers, each led by a light cruiser, to clear the way ahead of the bombardment force. These forces were deployed just over 5nm ahead of the two heavy cruisers and *Kirishima*. Once the way was clear, the heavy ships would close the island and shell the airfield into oblivion.

Lee was handicapped by the makeshift nature of his Task Force 64. None of his ships had ever operated together before so his battle plan had to be simple. He led his force on a sweep counterclockwise around Savo Island in order to cover both entrances into Iron Bottom Sound. The four destroyers, only two of which had radar, were deployed 5,000yd ahead of the battleships. The two battleships followed, with *Washington* leading and *South Dakota* 2,000yd behind. The best intelligence that Lee possessed was a report at 1700hrs that a Japanese force of four heavy cruisers, one large destroyer, and ten destroyers was closing Guadalcanal at high speed.

This early-1942 overhead view of *South Dakota* shows her stubby appearance when compared to the *North Carolina* class, which had a hull almost 50ft longer. Note the three 16in/45 triple turrets and the secondary battery. *South Dakota* was the sole ship of her class to possess only four 5in/38 mounts per side – the rest of the class had five.

USN ORDER OF BATTLE, BATTLESHIP DUEL OFF GUADALCANAL

Battleship Force (Rear Admiral Willis A. Lee, Jr. on *Washington*)
Washington (Captain Glenn Davis)
South Dakota (Captain Thomas Gatch)

Screen
Destroyers *Walke*, *Benham*, *Preston*, *Gwin*

IJN ORDER OF BATTLE, BATTLESHIP DUEL OFF GUADALCANAL

Bombardment Unit (Vice Admiral Kondō Nobutake on *Atago*)
Battleship *Kirishima* (Captain Iwabuchi Sanji)
Heavy cruisers *Atago*, *Takao*
Light cruiser *Nagara* (with Rear Admiral Kimura Susumu, commander of Destroyer Squadron 10)
Destroyers *Ikazuchi*, *Samidare*

Direct Escort Unit (Rear Admiral Takama Tamotsu on *Asagumo*)
Destroyers *Asagumo*, *Shirayuki*, *Hatsuyuki*, *Teruzuki*

Sweeping Unit (Rear Admiral Hashimoto Shintarō on *Sendai*)
Light cruiser *Sendai*
Destroyers *Ayanami*, *Shikinami*, *Uranami*

THE BATTLE DEVELOPS

None of the Japanese ships carried radar, but it was the Japanese that gained first contact. At 2313hrs, lookouts on the destroyer *Shikinami*, using their special night binoculars, spotted Lee's force east of Savo Island heading south. The Japanese ships were steering the same general course so were in the radar blind spot to the rear of the American formation. Rear Admiral Hashimoto Shintarō, leading the Sweeping Unit, reported to Kondō by 2328hrs that the American formation included two heavy cruisers and that he was maintaining contact. Contact on the Americans was temporarily lost in a rain squall, but the Japanese were able to track the USN force as it changed course to the west at 2352hrs. In response, Kondō ordered his heavy ships to change course to the northeast at 0015hrs to give the screening units time to deal with the Americans.

When the Americans changed course to the west, the Sweeping Unit was no longer in Lee's radar blind spot. *Washington* gained radar contact at 0001hrs on the Japanese force to the north at 18,000yd. This was followed by a visual contact at 0012hrs; two minutes later, Lee gave permission for his battleships to engage the targets thinking that this was the main Japanese bombardment force. The largest target, probably *Sendai*, was fired on at 0017hrs at 18,500yd by *Washington*'s main battery. Three salvos were fired, but after the second and third straddled the target, the splashes made the target disappear on radar. *South Dakota* opened fire a minute later, firing eight 16in salvos at the destroyer *Shikinami*. The secondary batteries on both battleships engaged destroyers. This engagement showed the limitations of firing by radar. Despite *Washington* firing 42 16in and some 100 5in shells, and *South Dakota*'s eight salvos of 16in shells, none of the three Japanese ships was hit.

The next phase of the action featured the destroyer *Ayanami* which had detached from the Sweeping Unit to conduct a solo counterclockwise sweep around Savo Island. When *Ayanami* reached a point south of Savo Island, she was detected by the radar on the lead American destroyer and then engaged by two destroyers and *Washington*'s secondary battery. *Ayanami* began a single-handed torpedo attack on Task Force 64 at 0024hrs. The destroyer launched six torpedoes at 0030hrs, which minutes later hit destroyers *Preston* and *Walke*. *Ayanami* also scored 5in-gun hits on *Gwin*. *Ayanami*'s brave attack made her the focus of return fire, and she took several 5in shells which set the destroyer on fire and soon caused a loss of power which brought her to a stop.

Right behind *Ayanami* was the light cruiser *Nagara* and her destroyers. Three American destroyers engaged *Nagara* shortly after she was spotted at 0027hrs, but were unable to score any hits. *Nagara* returned fire with her 5.5in guns and turned *Preston* into a shambles. At 0035hrs, *Nagara* and several destroyers executed a torpedo attack on Task Force 64 and then turned away. This torpedo salvo finished off the American destroyer screen. *Preston* was already a burning wreck, and at 0037hrs *Benham* was struck in the bow by a torpedo and placed out of action. *Walke* was struck by gunfire and then a torpedo; she quickly broke in two and sank. *Benham* and *Gwin* were ordered by Lee to clear the area. This left the two battleships as the only operational American units.

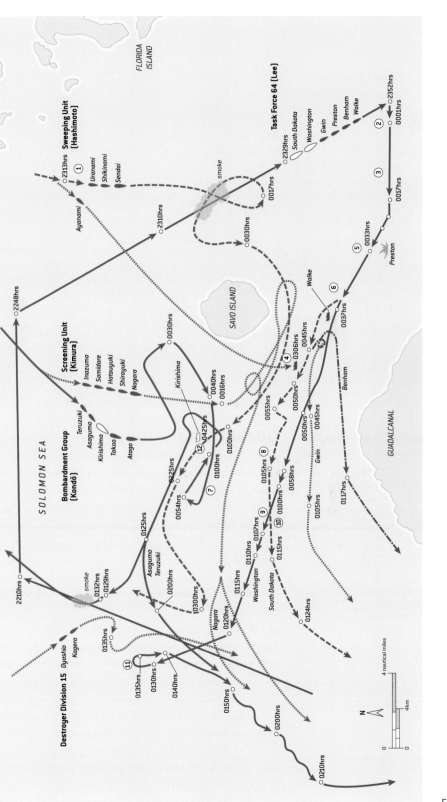

November 14

1. 2313hrs: Lee's force spotted by Japanese destroyer *Shikinami*.

November 15

2. 0001hrs: *Washington* gains radar contact on Japanese Sweeping Unit.

3. 0017hrs: *Washington* opens fire with her main battery against the Sweeping Unit and is joined by *South Dakota* one minute later; neither scores a hit.

4. 0030hrs: Japanese destroyer *Ayanami* launches torpedoes that hit two USN destroyers; *Ayanami* is hit by USN battleship and destroyer gunfire, set afire, and later sinks.

5. 0033hrs: *South Dakota* begins to experience electrical problems which plague her for the remainder of the battle.

6. 0037hrs: American destroyers *Benham* and *Walke* are hit by torpedoes; Lee's destroyer screen is gone.

7. 0050hrs: Japanese heavy cruiser *Takao* spots Lee's battleships.

8. 0100–0104hrs: Five Japanese ships, including *Kirishima*, pound *South Dakota* with at least 26 hits.

9. 0100–0107hrs: *Washington* hits *Kirishima* with 16in shells, inflicting fatal damage.

10. 0110hrs: *South Dakota* withdraws.

11. 0133hrs: *Washington* withdraws after escaping damage from dozens of Japanese torpedoes.

12. 0425hrs: *Kirishima* sinks.

SOLOMON SEA

FLORIDA ISLAND

SAVO ISLAND

GUADALCANAL

Bombardment Group (Kondō)

Screening Unit (Kimura)

Sweeping Unit (Hashimoto)

Task Force 64 (Lee)

Destroyer Division 15

THE BATTLESHIP DUEL

As the American destroyer screen disintegrated, the two battleships tried to make sense out of the confusing situation. Between 0030hrs and 0033hrs, *South Dakota* fired five salvos at *Sendai* to the north with no success. The shock tripped a circuit breaker on *South Dakota* which led to a loss of power. This meant that all radars were down which blinded the battleship. For the rest of the action, electrical power on *South Dakota* was intermittent. *Washington* continued on a course to the northwest and came upon the shattered destroyer screen. To the northwest, her radar picked up four contacts at 0035hrs. These were *Kirishima*, *Atago*, *Takao*, and one of the two escorting destroyers. One of the contacts was larger than the others which the main-battery plot began to track.

Kondō was encouraged by the reports from *Ayanami* and Rear Admiral Kimura Susumu on *Nagara* that several American cruisers and destroyers had been sunk or damaged. The report at 0045hrs from *Ayanami* that the destroyer had sunk a cruiser and a destroyer while damaging another caused elation on the bridge of *Atago*. This celebration was short-lived, however, since minutes later a report was received from *Sendai* that *Ayanami* was on fire. At 0050hrs, Kondō ordered another course change to the northwest to give the screening elements more time to mop up the Americans. It was at this time that the Japanese got their first glimpse of the two American battleships when *Takao*'s lookouts issued a report on a battleship and three destroyers to the south. At 0051hrs, Kimura warned Kondō that two battleships were heading west. Kondō dismissed both of these reports. He remained convinced he was facing

heavy cruisers, and that these had already been dealt with. At 0051hrs he ordered the Bombardment Force to head to the southeast in preparation for opening fire on the airfield.

As *Atago* headed for Lunga Point at 0055hrs, leading *Takao* and *Kirishima*, lookouts on *Atago* spotted *South Dakota* to port less than 6,000yd away. *Atago* immediately fired eight Type 93 torpedoes at 0059hrs but all missed. At 0100hrs, *Atago's* searchlights painted *South Dakota*, and all five Japanese ships of the bombardment force opened fire. For the next four minutes, Japanese gunfire ravaged *South Dakota*. From relatively short range, the well-trained Japanese gun crews scored heavily. The actual count and types of shells which struck the battleship remains unclear, but *South Dakota's* damage report indicates 18 8in, six 6in, one 5in, and a single 14in shell hit the ship.

The Japanese claimed *South Dakota* as sunk; in reality, the damage never threatened to sink the battleship. No shells penetrated her armored citadel. The most extensive damage was to the superstructure, knocking out radar and fire-control equipment. The damage was much less severe than it might have been since *Kirishima* fired a small percentage of armor-piercing shells and because most of the projectiles that hit the superstructure passed through without detonating. In return, *South Dakota* managed to get off five salvos from her main battery. With her main-battery fire-control director down, however, these failed to hit anything. Her 5in/38 guns were much more active, but again did not hit anything. At 0110hrs, Captain Gatch, with no functional radios or fire-control equipment, decided to withdraw.

While *South Dakota* was being pummeled by fire, *Washington* remained unnoticed by the Japanese. She had been tracking *Kirishima* and was ready to engage her by 0040hrs. Since the position of *South Dakota* was unclear, Lee denied his flagship permission to fire. Now, as the ordeal of *South Dakota* unfolded to observers on *Washington*, and with the position of *South Dakota* firmly established, Lee gave *Washington* permission to engage the large target to the northwest at 0100hrs. *Washington's* 16in/45 guns opened fire on *Kirishima* at 8,400yd – practically point-blank range for these powerful weapons. The main battery used radar to engage, but the shell splashes could not be distinguished on radar, so this had to be done optically. *Washington* got off two salvos before *Kirishima* was able to respond about a minute later.

In just 150 seconds, 39 16in shells were sent toward *Kirishima*. The first salvo was a straddle, according to both American and Japanese observers. The second salvo included a single hit on the forward superstructure on the compass bridge. The third salvo was observed to hit amidships and caused large, bright explosions according to an American observer. According to Japanese sources, as many as four hits were scored in this area, which caused large fires and contributed to the eventual loss of power. Two more hits were scored below the waterline which began to flood the ship. By the fourth salvo, the range between the two battleships was only 7,850yd. Two hits from this salvo struck *Kirishima*'s forward 14in/45 turret, knocking it out.

After these initial devastating salvos, Lee received a report that the target was sunk, so ordered a ceasefire. This pause lasted 90 seconds. When the report was shown to be erroneous, fire resumed for another 165 seconds during which a further 39 16in projectiles were sent downrange. Five more hits were probably placed forward, including another two below the waterline. *Kirishima* was heading north, presenting her stern to *Washington*, so most of the later hits were on her stern area. All hits were on the starboard side. *Washington* ceased fire at 0107hrs after firing a total of 75 16in and 107 5in shells at *Kirishima* and 120 5in shells at the two heavy cruisers.

An American observer saw three of *Kirishima*'s four turrets firing back initially, but her action was ineffective. After *Washington*'s resumption of fire, only *Kirishima*'s aft 14in/45 turret was observed to be firing. The nearest she came to hitting *Washington* was 200yd off her port quarter.

THE LATER PHASES

Following her encounter with *Washington*, *Kirishima* fell out of line and began to circle. The ship was on fire amidships and on her stern and was unable to maneuver since her steering compartment was partially flooded and her rudder jammed. Most devastating was severe flooding caused by 16in-shell strikes below the waterline which resulted in a starboard list. The fires were put out by 0349hrs, but the ship continued to be unnavigable. By now, the steering compartment was completely flooded, and attempts to steer with her engines were unsuccessful. At 0425hrs, *Kirishima* rolled over to port and sank with the loss of 212 of her crew. Another 1,218 crewmen were saved by destroyers.

As *Kirishima* was in her death throes, *Washington* continued to lead a charmed life. She had already evaded eight torpedoes from *Atago* and another four from the destroyer *Asagumo*. At 0113hrs, *Atago* and *Takao* each fired eight torpedoes at *Washington* from a range of only 4,000yd. Again, none hit the battleship which was unaware of the torpedo attack and still on a steady course. At least three more destroyers and *Nagara* also fired torpedoes at *Washington*, but some well-timed evasive maneuvers and Lee's continuing luck prevented any damage. By the end of the battle, *Atago* had fired 19 torpedoes, and *Takao* 20. Remarkably, none of the dozens of Japanese torpedoes aimed at *Washington* found its target.

Lee had been steaming to the west to locate and engage the last four ships of the Japanese troop convoy. He was unsuccessful in this, but he did delay the convoy enough so that it would have to unload during daylight hours. Having accomplished his mission, Lee withdrew from the area to the west of Guadalcanal at 0133hrs. At 0400hrs, the last four transports of the convoy were beached on the island and their

Washington was not damaged at Guadalcanal, but did suffer serious damage after colliding with the battleship *Indiana* during the Marshalls operation on February 1, 1944. Her bow was crushed and the battleship is shown here alongside a repair ship for initial attention. Following repairs, *Washington* rejoined the fleet in time to participate in the Battle of the Philippine Sea, the Battle of Leyte Gulf, and the invasions of Luzon, Iwo Jima, and Okinawa. *Washington* was placed out of commission in June 1947 and was in reserve until May 1961 when she was sold for scrapping.

cargoes began to be unloaded. After daybreak, American aircraft and a destroyer finished off these ships and destroyed the supplies which had been hastily unloaded onto the beach. The battle was over, and Lee and his flagship had emerged victorious.

SURIGAO STRAIT

Following the Guadalcanal campaign, USN battleships settled into a predictable pattern. The modern battleships were assigned to the Fast Carrier Task Force where their significant antiaircraft capabilities were highly prized. Because the IJN did not mount a significant fleet operation until June 1944, the fast battleships were not given a chance to engage surface targets. The only exception was on February 17, 1944 during the first carrier raid on the major Japanese base at Truk Atoll during which *Iowa* and *New Jersey* were dispatched to intercept IJN units attempting to escape from the air raid. *Iowa* engaged a Japanese training cruiser with 46 16in and 124 5in rounds and *New Jersey* engaged a destroyer with her secondary battery. Both IJN ships were sunk, but the battleships were not a factor in their demise. Later that same day, both battleships engaged a fleeing Japanese destroyer at ranges between 32,300yd and 39,000yd with a total of 58 16in shells. At this extreme range, the longest ever for a battleship, radar was used for ranging and spotting. The target was straddled, but not hit, and the destroyer escaped after firing torpedoes at her tormenters. This was the only occasion during the war that an Iowa-class battleship engaged a surface target.

The major fleet action in June 1944, the Battle of the Philippine Sea, was entirely a carrier battle. The 14 USN battleships present (seven modern ships assigned to the carriers and seven old battleships assigned to provide direct cover to the landing on Saipan in the Marianas) did not come close to engaging the five IJN battleships which

Musashi is shown under attack by USN carrier aircraft on October 24, 1944 in the Sibuyan Sea. This was the USN's first real encounter with one of the IJN's superbattleships. Her well-trained damage-control personnel and immense size made for a prolonged death – USN carrier aircraft hit her with 15 torpedoes and 16 bombs before sinking her. *Musashi* never fired her main armament in anger during her brief career of a little over two years, demonstrating the almost total failure of the IJN's battleships during the war.

were all operating with the Japanese carrier force. The fast battleships were formed into a separate task group and operated in advance of the main carrier force in expectation of a possible major surface engagement, but never got close to the Japanese. However, the next major American invasion in the Pacific prompted the IJN to make a supreme effort to defend the Philippines. The Japanese had determined that if the Philippines were lost, the vital artery from the resource-rich areas in the Dutch East Indies to Japan would be severed, representing a fatal blow to any prospects for a successful continuation of the war. To respond to the invasion of Leyte in October 1944, every major warship in the IJN was committed, including all nine remaining battleships. Since the IJN's carrier force had been shattered at the Battle of the Philippine Sea, the centerpiece of the Japanese plan was to get its heavy forces, including up to seven battleships, into Leyte Gulf to destroy the American landing force.

For a number of reasons, this plan was fatally flawed, not the least of which was that by the time the Japanese battleships could actually arrive in Leyte Gulf from their starting point from an anchorage in the Singapore area, the USN's amphibious force would be long gone and the invasion force safely ashore with an immense amount of supplies. In addition, the Japanese plan was very complex and dependent on good communications and coordination, which was unlikely to be the case during the actual operation. The focus of the operation was to get a force of seven battleships, 11 heavy cruisers, two light cruisers, and 19 destroyers into Leyte Gulf. This force was divided into two groups. The largest, with five battleships (*Yamato*, *Musashi*, *Nagato*, *Kongō*, and *Haruna*), ten heavy cruisers, two light cruisers, and 15 destroyers, planned to reach Leyte Gulf by way of the Sibuyan Sea, transiting San Bernardino Strait, and then transiting south along the coast of Samar Island. The exploits of this force will not be detailed since they did not involve a clash with USN battleships. To cover them briefly, on October 24 it underwent heavy air attacks from USN carrier aircraft in the Sibuyan Sea during which *Musashi* was sunk. This took an amazing total of 15 torpedo and 16 bomb hits to achieve. The force successfully exited San Bernardino Strait early on October 25, transited south toward Leyte, and encountered a large force of USN escort carriers off Samar Island. In a confused action, the Japanese sank one escort carrier, two destroyers, and a destroyer escort. In exchange, three Japanese heavy cruisers were lost. The four IJN battleships in this action shot poorly and contributed little. Following this encounter, the Japanese retreated back through San Bernardino Strait, barely avoiding the USN's Fast Carrier Task Force with its six modern battleships.

The actions of the rest of the First Diversion Attack Force (also known as Force "C") featured the last battleship action of the Pacific War. This force was ordered to enter Leyte Gulf from the south through Surigao Strait on the morning of October 25. Opposing this force was the 7th Fleet, which was providing direct support to the Leyte invasion. The two sides were unequally matched, making this more of a maritime execution than a battle. In addition to superior numbers, the USN had the benefit of a superior position since it was defending a choke point.

The Japanese force was commanded by Vice Admiral Nishimura Shōji. His plan was simple – he intended to rush into Leyte Gulf to take pressure off the main force approaching Leyte Gulf from the north. Kinkaid's plan was also simple. He placed his six battleships at the head of the strait, and south of them he deployed his eight cruisers in two flanking groups. With the strait only 12nm wide at this point, there was no possibility of the Japanese transiting through undetected. In advance of the heavy ships were three squadrons of destroyers tasked to make radar-guided torpedo attacks. Thirty-nine PT boats operated in the southern approaches to the strait to report the movements of the Japanese and make torpedo attacks where possible. The only potential problem for Kinkaid and

Yamashiro photographed under air attack from aircraft from the carrier *Enterprise* on the morning of October 24 in the Sulu Sea. Only near-misses were achieved which caused minor flooding. *Fusō* suffered more severe damage, but both battleships were able to continue to their fateful rendezvous in Surigao Strait with the USN.

USN ORDER OF BATTLE, SURIGAO STRAIT
Battleships: *West Virginia, Maryland, Tennessee, California, Mississippi, Pennsylvania*
Heavy cruisers: *Louisville, Portland, Minneapolis, Shropshire* (Australian)
Light cruisers: *Denver, Columbia, Phoenix, Boise*
Destroyers: 28
PT boats: 39

IJN ORDER OF BATTLE, SURIGAO STRAIT
Battleships: *Fusō, Yamashiro*
Heavy cruiser: *Mogami*
Destroyers: *Asagumo, Michishio, Yamagumo, Shigure*

his battle commander, Rear Admiral Jesse B. Oldendorf, was the shortage of battleship and cruiser armor-piercing shells since the majority of each ship's load-out was high explosive for shore bombardment. To make these shells count, it was decided that the battleships would not open fire until the Japanese closed to between 17,000yd and 20,000yd.

THE APPROACH PHASE

The battle began at 2236hrs on October 24 when a PT boat gained radar contact on Nishimura's force headed into the strait. In a series of actions lasting until 0213hrs on October 25, the PT boats conducted a number of harassing attacks, with many launching torpedoes. The Japanese fought off all attacks and maintained good order while moving up the strait. The next phase of Kinkaid's ambush was much more deadly.

Destroyer Squadron 54 brought seven large Fletcher-class destroyers to the fight. The squadron commander planned for five of these to attack the Japanese force from two directions using radar. Three destroyers launched a total of 27 torpedoes in the first attack. At 0308hrs, one torpedo – probably two, based on survivor accounts – hit *Fusō*. The second group of two destroyers fired a full salvo of 20 torpedoes at a favorable angle. Three hit *Yamagumo* which blew up and sank; one hit *Michishio* which left her crippled; another hit *Asagumo* on the bow. All these came from the destroyer *McDermut*, giving her the honor of firing the most effective USN destroyer torpedo salvo of the war.

Yamashiro did not escape damage. One torpedo from the destroyer *Monssen* hit the ship on her port side. The attacks of Destroyer Squadron 54 were more effective than Kinkaid could have reasonably hoped for. All but two of Nishimura's ships were hit; three were sinking and out of the battle. Following the initial torpedo attacks, Destroyer Squadron 24 with six destroyers gained another torpedo hit on *Yamashiro* at 0334hrs. The hit reduced her speed temporarily to 5kts, but within minutes engineers aboard had restored steam and the ship was back up to 18kts.

The first phase of the battle left Nishimura with only three ships to continue north into the face of Kinkaid's battle line. While *Yamashiro* was able to shake off two torpedo hits and keep moving, the damage to *Fusō* was fatal. After taking two torpedoes, she fell out of line and headed south. According to her few survivors, she sank by the bow at 0345hrs. Their accounts contradict the generally accepted version that she blew apart into two halves with each remaining afloat. In any event, *Fusō*'s demise meant the end of 1,630 sailors with only ten survivors reaching Japan.

THE GUNNERY PHASE

Radar operators on the American battleships and cruisers at the head of the strait followed the progress of Nishimura's diminished force. First radar contact was gained at 0323hrs at a range of 33,000yd. Waiting for the Japanese to close, the USN cruisers did not open fire until 0351hrs at a range of approximately 16,000yd. The first battleship to open fire was *West Virginia* two minutes later from 22,800yd. All ships fired at the largest radar return of the three Japanese ships which was *Yamashiro*.

The American battleship barrage grew as each ship developed a fire-control solution. *California* opened fire at 0355hrs from 20,400yd. *Tennessee* joined the fight a minute later. These were the three ships equipped with the Mk 8 fire-control radar.

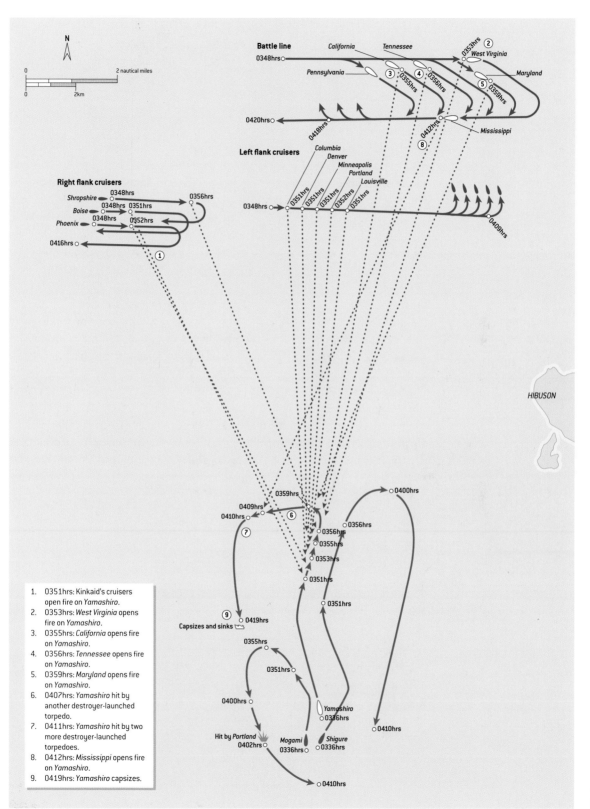

N

0 — 2 nautical miles
0 — 2km

Battle line

0348hrs

California *Tennessee* 0353hrs ② *West Virginia*

Pennsylvania ③ 0355hrs ④ 0356hrs *Maryland*

⑤ 0359hrs

0420hrs 0418hrs 0412hrs *Mississippi*

⑧

Left flank cruisers *Columbia*
Denver
Minneapolis
Portland
Louisville

0348hrs 0351hrs 0351hrs 0351hrs 0352hrs 0351hrs

0409hrs

Right flank cruisers

Shropshire 0348hrs 0356hrs
0348hrs 0351hrs
Boise 0348hrs
Phoenix 0348hrs 0352hrs

0416hrs

①

HIBUSON

0400hrs

0359hrs

0409hrs 0356hrs

0410hrs ⑥ 0356hrs

⑦ 0355hrs

0353hrs

0351hrs

0351hrs

⑨ 0419hrs

Capsizes and sinks

0355hrs

0351hrs

0400hrs

0410hrs

Yamashiro

0336hrs

Hit by *Portland*

0402hrs *Mogami* *Shigure*

0336hrs 0336hrs

0410hrs

1. 0351hrs: Kinkaid's cruisers
    open fire on *Yamashiro*.
2. 0353hrs: *West Virginia* opens
    fire on *Yamashiro*.
3. 0355hrs: *California* opens fire
    on *Yamashiro*.
4. 0356hrs: *Tennessee* opens fire
    on *Yamashiro*.
5. 0359hrs: *Maryland* opens fire
    on *Yamashiro*.
6. 0407hrs: *Yamashiro* hit by
    another destroyer-launched
    torpedo.
7. 0411hrs: *Yamashiro* hit by two
    more destroyer-launched
    torpedoes.
8. 0412hrs: *Mississippi* opens fire
    on *Yamashiro*.
9. 0419hrs: *Yamashiro* capsizes.

The other three battleships with the older Mk 3 struggled to gain a firing solution. At 0359hrs, *Maryland* opened fire by ranging with her Mk 3 radar on the splashes of the other battleships. *Mississippi* took longer to get into the fight. At 0412hrs, she fired a full salvo at *Yamashiro* from 19,790yd. This was the end of the battleship phase of the battle and was the final salvo in history of a battleship firing at another. *Pennsylvania* never gained a good solution for her 14in/45 main battery, so did not fire a single salvo.

Yamashiro put up a good fight in a hopeless situation. Hundreds of 6in, 8in, 14in, and 16in shells splashed around her; an unknown, but large, number hit according to witnesses from both sides. The battleship was ablaze in many locations, but returned fire from her main and secondary batteries. As early as 0356hrs, she had targeted the light cruiser *Phoenix*; at 0359hrs, the light cruiser *Columbia* observed near-misses. By 0401, she straddled the Australian heavy cruiser *Shropshire* with several salvos. The light cruiser *Denver* also came under fire. *Yamashiro*'s shooting was accurate and may have been assisted by radar, but no hits were scored by her 14in/45 guns.

The damage inflicted by the storm of American gunnery on *Yamashiro* was considerable, but the wounded battleship continued to move and shoot. *West Virginia* scored a hit with her first salvo on *Yamashiro*'s superstructure. Nishimura was not wounded, and remained on the bridge until the ship capsized. The blows which finally accounted for *Yamashiro* were delivered by Destroyer Squadron 56, the last USN destroyer squadron to attack. In the middle of the maelstrom of fire, nine destroyers closed to conduct torpedo and gunnery attacks. The last section put a torpedo into *Yamashiro*'s starboard engine room at 0407hrs. During a ceasefire ordered by Oldendorf at 0409hrs, *Yamashiro* turned south. At 0411hrs, two torpedoes from the destroyer *Newcomb* hit the battleship on her starboard side. In return, the destroyer *Albert W. Grant* was caught in the crossfire between the two sides. She took 19 hits, most from American 6in shells and at least six from *Yamashiro*'s secondary battery, and suffered 34 dead and 94 wounded.

Yamashiro's brave but futile fight came to an end at 0419hrs when the ship capsized to port. Only three survivors chose to be picked up by American ships. The

West Virginia in a floating dry dock at Espiritu Santo, New Hebrides in November 1944 following the Battle of Surigao Strait. Note the profusion of electronics and antiaircraft weaponry which were part of her rebuilding. The large torpedo blisters are also evident.

This photograph shows *Tennessee* in Buckner Bay, Okinawa, on July 17, 1945. This was her configuration during the Battle of Surigao Strait and clearly shows the extent of her rebuilding. Note the 14in/50 triple turrets and the dual 5in/38 dual-purpose mounts. The Mk 34 main-battery directors are clearly visible as is the Mk 8 radar fitted on top of them.

loss of life was again tremendous, totaling 1,636 crewmen – there were only ten survivors.

The heavy cruiser *Mogami* did not escape the withering American fire. After firing four Type 93 torpedoes, she came under fire from the heavy cruiser *Portland*. Two 8in shells hit *Mogami*'s bridge at 0402hrs, killing the commanding officer. Later in the action, *Mogami* suffered 10–20 6in and 8in hits while heading out of the strait, but remained afloat and it appeared that she might survive. The tough ship was later hit by 500lb bombs from USN escort carrier aircraft and was finally scuttled. Of Nishimura's force, only the destroyer *Shigure* survived.

The last phase of the action was anticlimactic. In another indication of the shambolic state of Japanese planning for the battle, a force under Vice Admiral Shima Kiyohide comprised of two heavy and one light cruiser and four destroyers was ordered to attack Leyte Gulf through Surigao Strait. The movement of Shima's force was not coordinated with Nishimura's force. The second force appeared in the strait after Nishimura's destruction, a fact of which – incredibly – Shima was ignorant, since Nishimura had failed to inform him of the battle's progress. After arriving in the strait and seeing the burning remains of Nishimura's force, and having one of his heavy cruisers rammed by the wounded *Mogami* heading south, Shima decided to abort his mission. His only contribution to the battle was to fire 16 Type 93 torpedoes up the strait which hit nothing. The final battleship clash in history had ended in a resounding American victory.

Maryland never received an extensive modernization during the war. This view shows her following an overhaul in April 1944 and illustrates her configuration when she fought at Surigao Strait. *Maryland* was never fitted with a Mk 8 fire-control radar, limiting her effectiveness in a surface engagement.

STATISTICS AND ANALYSIS

BATTLESHIP DUEL OFF GUADALCANAL

Lee's victory at the Second Naval Battle of Guadalcanal was in many ways unlikely. In a night battle, he was unable fully to exploit his biggest asset – the range of his 16in guns. The immaturity of American radars of the period meant that the action would probably be conducted at fairly close range. If this had been the case, then the torpedo tactics of the Japanese and their excellent Type 93 torpedo with its 1,078lb warhead and a remarkable range of up to 43,700yd at 36kts might have been the determining factors.

The first phase of the battle went entirely Kondō's way. As on several occasions during the Guadalcanal campaign, Japanese optics outperformed American electronics, allowing the IJN to gain first contact on Lee's force. When Lee unleashed his battleships to engage the Sweeping Unit at a range of 18,500yd at 0017hrs, it was the first occasion in the Pacific that the USN employed its 16in guns in anger. In spite of the optimistic reports from the main-battery plot that the targets had been destroyed, no Japanese ship was hit. As the battle developed, the aggressive Japanese accounted for the entire USN destroyer screen through a combination of torpedoes and gunnery. In comparison, no American destroyer got a single torpedo into the water. The only Japanese loss was the destroyer *Ayanami* which was sunk by gunfire, including probably by *South Dakota*'s secondary battery using radar control – the only hit scored by *South Dakota* during the entire battle.

Lee's victory was solely due to radar, as he acknowledged after the battle. When presented with a large target at fairly short range, *Washington* shot well. The opening range to *Kirishima* was 8,400yd which made for a deadly outcome. *Washington*'s gun crews rocked salvos back and forth over *Kirishima*. The Mk 3 radar was excellent in providing range, which meant that the Americans did not have to bracket the target before firing for effect. Even with radar, hitting a moving target at range is difficult, as the table below illustrates clearly. Only *Washington* enjoyed any real degree of success during the battle, when she engaged *Kirishima* at fairly close range.

ABOVE LEFT
Taken from her USN damage report, this is the result of a 6in or 8in hit on the hull of *South Dakota*. The shell hit amidships on a fuel and ballast tank and exploded on contact. Note the sheared rivets and the fragment holes in the interior plating.

ABOVE RIGHT
Another photograph of the damage to *South Dakota*. This was caused by an 8in shell that hit forward and created a 4×5ft hole.

USN battleship gunnery at the Second Naval Battle of Guadalcanal

Ships involved	Total rounds fired/hits	
	16in rounds	5in rounds
South Dakota (during the entire action)	115/0	115/0
Washington at Sweeping Unit	42/0	100/0 (approximately)
Washington at *Ayanami*	0/0	133/probably several
Washington at *Kirishima*	75/20	107/17
Washington at *Atago* and *Takao*	0/0	120/2 (on *Atago*)

It is impossible to reconstruct the damage to *Kirishima* definitively. What is clear is that all of the damage was inflicted by *Washington* between 0100hrs and 0107hrs. The standard account of the damage to *Kirishima* has been provided by Lieutenant Commander Horishi Tokuno, who in a postwar interrogation stated that *Kirishima* was hit by nine 16in shells and 40 5in shells. Lee's after-action report stated that *Kirishima* was hit by eight 16in shells. The total of 16in hits seems too low based on other sources, and the total of 40 5in hits out of 107 fired seems too high.

A more realistic account is provided by Lieutenant Commander Hayashi Shiro, *Kirishima*'s Chief Damage Control Officer. Before the ship sank, he created a sketch of the damage to his ship. It shows a total of 20 16in hits and 17 5in hits and is used in the table above. Whatever the final number of 16in-shell hits, *Kirishima*'s protective scheme lacked the ability to defeat them at that range. The damage included several underwater hits which led to severe flooding and caused *Kirishima's* sinking only a few hours later.

This was one of only two occasions during World War II when a battleship was sunk under way solely by projectiles fired from another battleship (the other occasion being the sinking of *Hood* by *Bismarck* in May 1941). This was testimony to the destructive power of the 2,700lb shell fired from a 16in naval rifle and its ability to penetrate the weak armor of a Kongō-class battleship. When the battle came down to a contest between *Kirishima*, a design dating from 1911 with no radar, and *Washington*, commissioned just a year earlier in 1941 and fitted with the most modern fire-control radar afloat, the outcome was never in doubt.

In comparison, *Kirishima* fared poorly against *South Dakota*. According to one Japanese source, *Kirishima* fired 117 14in rounds against the American battleship. In addition, *Atago* fired 61 8in rounds and *Takao* 36 at the same target. The official USN damage report for *South Dakota* stated that she was subjected to 26 hits and that only one of these was from a 14in shell. This hit the barbette of Turret 3 and did not penetrate, but blew a hole in the main deck around the barbette. Most of the damage on *South Dakota* was to her superstructure, but one shell hit below the waterline and two near the waterline which caused minor flooding. At no time was the ship in danger of sinking and no serious fires were started. The USN report stated that 18 of the hits were from 8in shells. The two Japanese heavy cruisers fired 97 8in rounds, which would represent an extraordinary accuracy rate. It is likely that some of the hits identified as 8in were actually from 14in shells since only 27 of the 117 rounds fired by *Kirishima* were armor-piercing; high-explosive and incendiary shells could cause damage mistaken for that of a smaller shell. Japanese sources claim as many as ten hits from *Kirishima* on *South Dakota*, but this also seems unlikely.

Though the battle was decided by the unequal duel between *Washington* and *Kirishima*, it could have been otherwise. Blessed with a fine performance by *Washington*, which single-handedly won the battle, Lee also came into more than his fair share of luck. His screen accomplished nothing, and soon after his destroyers were neutralized, *South Dakota* was taken out of action by a combination of equipment failure and enemy action. Not fully aware of the Japanese torpedo threat from the long-range Type 93, Lee steered *Washington* on a steady course for much of the action. In battles before and after this encounter, this was a recipe for total disaster. On this occasion, however, despite the Japanese firing dozens of torpedoes at *Washington*, many at fairly short range and at favorable angles, none hit their target. Had any of them done so, this almost certainly would have changed the course of the battle. If any had done so early in the battle, Kondō would possibly have had the opportunity to press on with his bombardment mission, which could have resulted in the neutralization of Henderson Field.

This hypothetical case for Japanese victory at the Second Naval Battle of Guadalcanal has to include a discussion of the overall situation. This addresses the question of whether the role played by Lee's battleships was decisive or not. It has to be kept in mind that the all-out effort overseen by the commander of the Combined Fleet, Marshal Admiral Yamamoto Isoruku, had been terribly mismanaged. The bulk of the large convoy headed to Guadalcanal had been destroyed the day before the

battleship clash on the night of November 14–15. Thus, even if Kondō had been able to bombard and neutralize the airfield, the remnant of the convoy actually able to reach Guadalcanal unmolested would not have provided the Japanese garrison on the island with a decisive edge. Nevertheless, the destruction of almost the entire convoy between November 14–15 and the loss of two Japanese battleships within three days brought an end to Japanese attempts to reinforce the island. In this sense, the Naval Battles of Guadalcanal fought between November 12 and November 15 were decisive, as was the role of USN battleships. The question needs to be asked: if the role of American battleships was decisive, why did Yamamoto not bring his heavier battleships into play? While purely hypothetical, the appearance of *Yamato* off Lunga Point could have provided the IJN with the firepower to guarantee the destruction of the airfield. While Halsey threw all caution to the wind and committed *Washington* and *South Dakota* in the most unfavorable conditions imaginable, Yamamoto kept his most modern battleships in Truk Atoll from where they played no role in the battle.

This photograph is from November 1942 and shows *South Dakota* and two destroyers alongside a repair ship, probably at Noumea, New Caledonia. After initial attention, *South Dakota* proceeded to the United States for complete repairs. Once complete, she operated in the Atlantic during February–August 1943, including service with the British Home Fleet. She returned to the Pacific and took part in the Gilberts and Marshalls invasions during November 1943–February 1944. *South Dakota* participated in the Battle of the Philippine Sea, during which she was hit by a bomb on June 19, but suffered only light damage. The battleship was also present at Leyte Gulf, and the invasions of Leyte, Luzon, Iwo Jima, and Okinawa. She shelled targets in the Japanese Home Islands in July and August 1945. The veteran battleship was decommissioned in 1947, but never again saw active service before being scrapped in 1962.

SURIGAO STRAIT

By 1944, the IJN had no chance of turning the tide of battle. Nevertheless, it made a supreme effort to do so at Leyte Gulf in October. In the series of actions that made up this battle, the most hopeless from the Japanese perspective was the Battle of Surigao Strait. The IJN did not perform well at Surigao Strait, a marked difference from the Japanese performance in night battles earlier in the war. Though all major Japanese ships were equipped with radar by this point, there is no evidence it was used effectively at Surigao Strait. Their usual prowess with night optics was also not in evidence; on several occasions American destroyers closed for torpedo attacks from which the Japanese did not even initiate evasive maneuvers. The Japanese also lacked

aggressiveness. The destroyer *Shigure* left the battle having not fired a single torpedo, as was the case with the four destroyers of Shima's force. The performance of Nishimura's two old battleships was mixed. *Fusō* sank after taking two torpedoes, but *Yamashiro* took four probable torpedoes and withstood a veritable barrage of gunfire from 16in to 5in shells, and still kept firing back with some degree of accuracy.

In the end, Nishimura's prospects for success, just like the overall plan for the IJN at Leyte Gulf, were wholly unrealistic. The balance of forces and a failure to work with Shima made any prospects for success very remote. But the loss of Nishimura's entire force, except for a single destroyer, in exchange for the damage to a single American destroyer, speaks to the fact that by 1944 the IJN's fighting capabilities had severely diminished and it was no longer the force it had been at the beginning of the war.

The Americans devised a simple and solid plan to maximize their considerable numerical advantage. Kinkaid realized the dream of every surface-warfare officer by crossing the "T" of his opponent. Again, radar was the key for the Americans. Its widespread use provided them with an immense advantage in overall situational awareness and critical targeting data for torpedoes and guns.

While American torpedoes were the most effective weapon of the battle, the big guns of

PT-321 pictured picking up a Japanese survivor in Surigao Strait. The scale of the Japanese defeat in this battle was breathtaking. Of Nishimura's seven ships, only a single destroyer survived. Total personnel casualties reached almost 4,100 men.

the battleships also played an effective role. The capabilities of the USN's advanced fire-control systems were on full display. *West Virginia*, *California*, and *Tennessee* were all equipped with the Mk 8 fire-control radar. *West Virginia* began the big-gun phase of the battle by scoring a direct hit on *Yamashiro* with her first salvo. The three Mk 8-equipped ships fired the majority of the USN's large-caliber rounds in the battle; *West Virginia* 93, *Tennessee* 69, and *California* 63. Beyond the first-salvo hit scored by *West Virginia*, it is impossible to ascertain how many more large-caliber shells hit *Yamashiro*. The battleships carrying the older Mk 3 fire-control radar were much less effective. *Maryland* fired only 48 rounds probably with minimal accuracy since she was using the splashes of the other battleships as a target; *Mississippi* fired a single salvo of 12 rounds and *Pennsylvania* did not fire at all. Fire distribution was an issue since all the American battleships and initially all of the cruisers concentrated their fire on *Yamashiro* only.

CONCLUSION

It is remarkable that in almost four years of war in the Pacific, American and Japanese battleships met in battle only twice. Unfortunately for the Japanese, on both occasions their two oldest classes of battleships were thrust into battle. On both occasions, the use of radar was decisive, which highlighted one of the IJN's principal wartime weaknesses. The designs of the ships themselves were also important factors in the outcomes of the two battleship duels. Despite her extensive modernization, *Kirishima* was outclassed by 1942 and stood no chance against the modern USN battleships she encountered off Guadalcanal in 1942. The two ships of the Fusō class were also overwhelmed in Surigao Strait in 1944 where they were betrayed by their weak protection.

The three battleships of the New Mexico class never received comprehensive modernization during the Pacific War because of their commitments to support amphibious operations. This photograph shows *Mississippi* in January 1945 during the landings at Lingayen Gulf bombarding a target ashore. She is followed by *West Virginia* and the Australian heavy cruiser *Shropshire*.

A towering pillar of smoke marks the end of *Yamato* on April 7, 1945. The battleship was sent on a senseless mission to attack the American invasion force off Okinawa but was sunk 200nm short of her target. It took seven bombs and 9–12 torpedoes to sink her, demonstrating that no battleship could be armored sufficiently to withstand air attack.

The two battleship duels were emblematic of the overall lack of success enjoyed by the IJN's battleship force during the war. While the Kongō class saw considerable action, the IJN rarely used its other battleships. The fact which puts the success of the IJN's battleship force into perspective is that its most successful action of the entire war was during the bombardment of the airfield on Guadalcanal in October 1942, and not in a fleet action. At Leyte Gulf, the Japanese committed their entire remaining strength, including their last nine battleships. Of these, three were sunk and a fourth never returned to Japan. The five remaining were hunted down in 1945. *Yamato* met her end in a totally senseless mission to attack the American invasion force off Okinawa in April 1945, and three more were sunk in harbor. Only *Nagato* survived the ravages of USN carrier aircraft to be surrendered at war's end.

By contrast, USN battleships played active and effective roles throughout the war. The ten modern ships commissioned were an integral part of the Fast Carrier Task Force, though they were valued for their antiaircraft capabilities rather than their big guns which were rarely used. The old battleships did not possess the speed to participate in fleet actions, but were fully integrated into the USN's amphibious forces which conducted an unstoppable wave of assaults throughout the Pacific from 1943 until the end of the war. As gunfire-support ships the old battleships were unsurpassed, and they proved largely immune to the *kamikaze* storm which enveloped the USN from October 1944 on. The investment made by the USN in its battleship force paid off much more handsomely than did that of the IJN.

BIBLIOGRAPHY

Action Reports, *Washington* and *South Dakota*, Night of November 14–15, 1942.

Bureau of Ships, *U.S.S. South Dakota (BB57) Gunfire Damage*, June 1, 1947.

Campbell, John (2002). *Naval Weapons of World War Two*. Annapolis, MD: Naval Institute Press.

Friedman, Norman (1981). *Naval Radar*. Greenwich: Conway Maritime Press.

Friedman, Norman (1985). *U.S. Battleships*. Annapolis, MD: Naval Institute Press.

Friedman, Norman (2008). *Naval Firepower*. Annapolis, MD: Naval Institute Press.

Fuller, Richard (2011). *Japanese Admirals 1926–1945*. Atglen, PA: Schiffer Publishing.

Gregor, Rene (1997). *Battleships of the World*. Annapolis, MD: Naval Institute Press.

Morison, Samuel Eliot (1975a). *The Struggle for Guadalcanal August 1942–February 1943*. Volume V of History of United States Naval Operations in World War II. Boston, MA: Little, Brown & Co.

Morison, Samuel Eliot (1975b). *Leyte, June 1944–January 1945*. Volume XII of History of United States Naval Operations in World War II. Boston, MA: Little, Brown & Co.

O'Hara, Vincent P. (2007). *The U.S. Navy Against the Axis*. Annapolis, MD: Naval Institute Press.

Stille, Mark (2008). *Imperial Japanese Battleships 1941–45*. Oxford: Osprey Publishing.

Stille, Mark (2013). *The Naval Battles for Guadalcanal 1942*. Oxford: Osprey Publishing.

Stille, Mark (2015a). *US Standard Type Battleships 1941–45 (1)*. Oxford: Osprey Publishing.

Stille, Mark (2015b). *US Standard Type Battleships 1941–45 (2)*. Oxford: Osprey Publishing.

Terzibaschitsch, Stefan (1977). *Battleships of the U.S. Navy in World War II*. New York, NY: Bonanza Books.

Tully, Anthony P. (2009). *Battle of Surigao Strait*. Bloomington, IN: Indiana University Press.

Whitley, M.J. (1998). *Battleships of World War Two*. Annapolis, MD: Naval Institute Press.

Yoshida Toshio (2004). *Shikikan-tachi no Taiheiyo Senso* (The Pacific War as Described by the Senior Officers). Tokyo: Kojinsha.

www.combinedfleet.com

INDEX

References to illustrations are shown in **bold**.